"Mark Vega, one of the most outstanding youth leaders in the Hispanic community in North America, offers what I consider a clear, biblical, and convincing answer to this very important issue. *Don't Wait for Me to Die* will be a powerful word for twenty-first century Christian leaders."

Dr. Saturnino Gonzalez
General Pastor
El Calvario Church, Orlando, Florida

"This is an amazing book that everyone must read. It will surely change your life!"

Mariano Rivera
New York Yankees Pitcher

DON'T WAIT
FOR ME TO
DIE

DON'T WAIT FOR ME TO DIE

MARK VEGA

GRUPO NELSON
Una división de Thomas Nelson Publishers
Desde 1798

NASHVILLE   DALLAS   MÉXICO DF.   RÍO DE JANEIRO   BEIJING

Translation: *Terry McDowell*
Design: *www.Blomerus.org*

ISBN: 978-1-60255-137-4

Printed in the United States of America

08 09 10 11 12 BTY 9 8 7 6 5 4 3 2 1

Contents

Dedication

This book is dedicated to my wife Lisa:
your consecration to the Lord and dedication
to me are impeccable.

And also to my mother: thank you for your determination
and faithfulness in raising me and navigating through the
storms until I reached God's mission for my life.

Introduction

Although we are more than conquerors in Jesus, this road is not easy. It has cost us pain, tears, and multiple scars. The enemy launches each attack with greater intensity, making us feel that we are in the last round and that the end is near. With every blow and every punch thrown against your ministry, your marriage, or your spiritual life, your energy and resistance is being diluted to the point of danger.

Paul finds himself bitten by a venomous viper. Instead of coming to his aid, those around him begin judging and accusing him. As if that were not enough, they watch closely, expecting him to soon fall over dead from the fatal bite. Can you identify with this? People see a dangerous viper hanging from your hand, and instead of helping they start diagnosing your situation. This lethal viper will most certainly cause your demise. There are vipers that have taken hold of us, and their poison has brought us almost to the brink of death.

The most dangerous viper is the one that sneaks in with such subtlety that we are not even aware of the attack. Look at your enemies: dressed in black, celebrating your funeral. They are preparing your grave, choosing the flowers, shining your casket. Everything is prepared for your burial. But they have forgotten that God has injected you with an antidote that will neutralize every diabolical attack—the Holy Spirit, who gives us immunity from Satan's fatal onslaughts. Now we can serve notice and boldly proclaim to the satanic kingdom and to our enemies: *Don't wait for me to die!*

MARK VEGA
JAN. 9, 1970 –

Chapter 1

The Four Seasons of Walking with God

It is extremely important that every believer understand that his walk with God is made up of different seasons. There are those who do not understand this concept and later make permanent decisions based on temporary circumstances. They believe that their situation—be it spiritual, emotional, physical, or financial—will never change. And convinced of this, they feel compelled to make decisions that are outside of God's will.

The enemy (Satan) takes advantage of a believer's insecurity and uncertainty for "he is a double-minded man, unstable in all his ways" (James 1:8).

It is impossible to define ourselves in our walk with Christ if we cannot discern where we are in life, or if we do not know where we are headed. "My people are destroyed for lack of knowledge" (Hos. 4:6).

Ignorance destroys. There are believers who have lived under a cloud of self-condemnation for the last twenty years because of making wrong decisions that caused them great losses in the Lord. Instead of progressing toward their destiny, they stop and condemn themselves. They are attacked by thoughts such as "What could I have been if . . .?" "Where would I have been today if . . .?" "What could I have done if . . .?" These kinds of thoughts only tend to dominate our minds and weaken our trust in God and ourselves. Satan seeks to infiltrate our life in one way or another, no matter how small or insignificant a thought might seem for the moment, in order to claim legal right over it. And once this is accomplished, the believer will then begin to walk, think, and live bound to carnal ideologies and concepts.

If we are not aware of God's overall plan (sometimes hidden) for our lives, it can cause us confusion, and in a subtle way we suffer opposition. At times we misinterpret God's voice and the direction He wants to give us, and unwittingly a spiritual war begins against God's plan and His will.

God allows certain changes, losses, and failures to occur, which are necessary for a complete development of our character and His plan for our lives.

It is essential to recognize the mission, plan, and calling that our God has for us. If we do not recognize His voice, we will never know what they are.

In its natural state, a diamond is simply known as coal. As such, it is something that lacks beauty or attractiveness. What transforms this stone into something desirable are the forces of heat and pressure that come upon it from the outside. After many decades of extreme heat and pressure, a change occurs within the stone, changing its inward molecular structure. This metamorphosis occurs from the inside out rather than from the outside inward. The only requirement the coal needs to gain more value and elegance is resistance. If it can withstand that intense pressure, then a total transformation happens. But the moment the coal breaks, the process is ruined, and it will never attain its fullness. However, if it can resist, enduring the needed process, the final product will be the most precious stone in the entire world: a diamond. The ugliness of the piece of coal disappears completely, and what remains, in exchange, is a radiant beauty.

At times, the process doesn't seem to make any sense, but

in the end we see the result, and we are glad for the change. "But we have this treasure in earthen vessels, that the excellence of the power may be of God and not of us" (2 Corinthians 4:7). As believers, we are exposed to experiences of sadness, weeping, afflictions, anxieties, weaknesses, and fears. In spite of these difficult moments, they are not a sign of defeat, but rather change and victory. In order to reach the fullness of God's plan for us, resistance, perseverance, and tenacity are necessary. If you give up during the process, you will be disqualified and will be incapable of attaining God's plan for your life.

God, our expert architect, allows certain oppositions and rivalries because He wants to design the characteristics of His people one person at a time: "We are hard-pressed on every side, yet not crushed; we are perplexed, but not in despair; persecuted, but not forsaken; struck down, but not destroyed" (2 Corinthians 4:8-9).

The farther you want the arrow to fly, the greater the tension must be on the bowstring. The archer pulls until he can pull no farther, then he aims and finally releases the arrow. In the same way, God sometimes pulls us back as far as He can, aims us toward our target, and then releases us so we can carry out His purposes. Many times we fight against it because we do not understand that we have been chosen for purposes so particular that only God knows. We must allow God to do with us whatever He deems appropriate. If we are in His hands, we will not suffer any harm.

The Four Seasons

Born and raised in New York, I enjoyed the four seasons of the year: summer, fall, winter, and spring. This cycle repeats itself every year without fail. As believers on our journey with God, we go through similar and important seasons.

Summer is a beautiful time. The sun's heat covers the whole earth. The seas reveal their splendor, and the trees produce their fruit. The leaves of the trees and the grass in the fields clothe themselves in their best color. The laughter of children can be heard, and their happiness spreads to others. During these months of summer, light dominates. The beaches and parks fill up with people who enjoy their leisure. It is a time of relaxation, peace, and joy. The mood of the environment spreads from person to person.

The "summer" of a believer begins when we become a new creature. Our new nature is an agreeable and pleasant time. We are in love with our Savior, and everything else is secondary. Our prayers seem to be heard and answered instantly. From the moment we open our eyes, we can feel God's overwhelming warmth. We see a real change in our character. Every time we read the Word, we feel God's presence, and we learn how to apply the scriptures to our own lives. This season is full of new experiences from the Lord. It is a time when God imparts new dreams to us, new visions, new encouragements, and new energies. Every day that goes by, we feel that God loves us more and more. This love can be seen as it spills over into every area of our lives. We receive promotions at work that before seemed impossible. Every day we thank God for life, for His favor, and for His grace that we can see living inside of us. New relationships develop with our brothers and sisters in the faith. We are surrounded by kind, cordial, and friendly people. These new experiences fill us with a security we have never felt before. God's fellowship and faithfulness have no equal. We are invited to countless celebrations, dinners, and times of fellowship. More and more people seem to take note of us each day, our "fame," begins to increase. We are sought after by new friends, and brothers and sisters in the Lord. We have never felt so special and so loved. Summer is a season we never want to end. The love, joy, and peace we feel are constant. The only difficult thing to do during this time is trying to stop smiling. From the moment the sun comes up and until it goes down, a constant stream of happiness splashes over us. Joy is constant. "He who is of a merry heart has a continual feast" (Proverbs 15:15).

After summer comes fall. The changes that come in this season are remarkable. The overwhelming heat disappears. The grass loses its greenness. The leaves change their color and fall from the trees, leaving them bare and lacking their natural beauty. Clouds cover the sun, and with that, the beautiful experiences in the Lord begin to decrease. The friendships that we formed during the summer begin to ebb. Those people (the leaves) that used to seek you out during the time of your "summer" now begin to change their minds. The social life you used to enjoy so much begins to diminish, as well as your brothers and sisters in the Lord who always used to be around you. Your prayers and petitions are no longer answered with the same quickness you experienced during the summertime. It is important to know that you must walk this path by faith and not by sight.

When winter arrives, the situation worsens. The cold and darkness invade day and night. The sun is hidden from our sight for most of the day. The trees lose their elegance, and they no longer produce fruit. The grass dries up and changes color. Nothing grows. Everything becomes dark. When rainstorms come and snow falls, the weather turns dangerous. Highway accidents increase because of ice-covered streets. In the same way, in the spiritual life of the believer, God's promises seem to die. We notice that in spite of our labor for the Lord, no growth or fruit can be seen. It is a time when we have to walk by pure faith. We feel the loneliness that surrounds us, and at times it seems we are very far from our God. But, take courage. It is in moments like these that we have to follow God no matter the cost. Although we may not see the solution to the problem that is attacking us, the answer to our petitions, the healing of a sickness, the restoration of our marriage, the financial provision, or the freedom from bondages, we can still trust in the God who is always faithful and all powerful.

Thank God that after winter comes spring. Springtime is a time of restoration. Everything that winter took from us we now repossess. The earth begins to wake up from its long sleep. We see how the temperature changes. The sun shines with all its strength and covers the earth again. A time of new growth comes, green foliage returns to the fields, fruits grow again; everything that seemed to have been lost is now recovered. God shows us His faithfulness. Whereas we believed that He had forgotten all about us, we now see His seal of approval. Our time is redeemed, and our faith seems to increase.

Meteorologists confirm that the different seasons of the year are beneficial for the healthy development of our planet. In a spiritual sense, these seasons are also important and profitable for our perfection.

Discussion Questions for Chapter 1

1. Think of a drastic decision that you have had to make in the last three months. Do you believe you made this decision according to God's will? If not, why?
2. Satan looks for a way to infiltrate our lives in one way or another to take advantage of us and to gain a legal right over us. What legal right do you think you have given to Satan, be it emotional, spiritual, or physical? How can you reclaim that legal right?
3. How long has it been since you last heard God's voice? How do you recognize the Master's voice? What do you think God has been trying to say to you?
4. God is always speaking, and He always answers our prayers. Do you pretend that God tells you what you want to hear? Are you satisfied with what God is telling you?
5. If we focus on the process that a piece of coal has to go through in order to be transformed into a diamond, we will notice that for this to be accomplished, it must

undergo extreme heat and pressure for a long time. What heat and pressures are you going through right now? Does your situation discourage you, or does the prospect of the final result encourage you?

6. The transition from being an immature Christian to a mature, spiritual Christian involves a lot of resistance. What kind of pressures are you experiencing at this moment? Do you regard these pressures with a negative attitude or a positive one? Are you happy when there aren't any problems or pressures that require your resistance? And when there are pressures, are you happy?

7. How do you view moments of affliction and difficulty? As a defeat or as an opportunity to overcome?

8. What spiritual season of life do you think you're in? What reasons make you believe this? (Be specific and personal.) Knowing that seasons have constant cycles, how can you prepare for what is coming next?

MARK VEGA

JAN. 9, 1970 -

Chapter 2

Take Heart

And now I urge you to take heart, for there will be no loss of life among you, but only of the ship. For there stood by me this night an angel of the God to whom I belong and whom I serve, saying, 'Do not be afraid, Paul; you must be brought before Caesar; and indeed God has granted you all those who sail with you.' Therefore take heart, men, for I believe God that it will be just as it was told me. (Acts 27:22-25)

It is essential to know how important it is for God to keep His Word. When the heroes of the faith would become discouraged, they remembered God's promises. They understood that if God had declared it, he would fulfill it. God and His Word cannot be separated. As long as God has a word and a purpose for a believer's life, and that believer is seeking God and following the direction of the Holy Spirit, the Lord will protect him from death. We should fight for God's promises because they are worthy to be received. Paul instructed Timothy to fight to see the fulfillment of all those prophecies. Timothy understood that in order to receive that which God had promised him, he had to fight the good fight (1 Timothy 1:18).

Perhaps you are asking yourself, why do I have to fight in order to obtain what God has already promised? It is because you will experience many types of opposition that will happen simultaneously. Every word that God speaks into your life will come to pass, but what determines its fulfillment will be your faith.

In our country, faith has turned into a luxury, something

that is not always necessary. In religious circles, the word *faith* has become a cliché, a simple saying. The prosperity in the United States has blinded believers; that's why many ask: Why do we need faith when we have everything at our fingertips? The reality is that the more we depend on our material resources, the less we are going to exercise our faith, which will shipwreck God's promises for our lives.

Storms are hurled at you by the enemy the moment God chooses you as His special vessel to use for His glory. In the Gospel of Mark, chapter 4, we read Jesus saying to his disciples: "Let us cross over to the other side" (v. 35). It is interesting to observe that the Bible says there were other boats; nevertheless, the only boat that was tossed about by the storm was the one Jesus had chosen, that one over which a prophetic word had been spoken. The boat destined to cross over to the other side, the one that was going to serve as a vehicle of fulfillment of what Jesus had declared, was being threatened by Satan's doing. The disciples believed they were going to drown. They did not know the purpose Jesus had planned for them. They allowed the storm to dictate their faith. They went and woke up Jesus, and the Lord immediately calmed the storm; but after the disciples had celebrated the Master's miracle, they were rebuked for their lack of faith.

Paul is also found doubting in a storm. The ship is breaking apart into pieces together with his faith. God, then, sends him an angel and informs him that it's necessary for him to appear before Caesar. Paul understands that he will survive because God will carry out His mission and His purpose. At times, the attack is so huge that it overshadows God's purpose for our lives.

During those times, you need to lift your sights and see beyond the present and discern that what is happening all around you doesn't even compare to what God will bring about in His perfect time. "For I consider that the sufferings of this present time are not worthy to be compared with the glory which shall be revealed in us" (Romans 8:18).

Don't focus too much on what has happened, whether storms, hurricanes, tsunamis, earthquakes, or floods. Look beyond the temporal, for there is a permanent plan God wants to fulfill in your life. "While we do not look at the things which are seen, but at the things which are not seen. For the things which are seen are temporary, but the things which are not seen are eternal" (2 Corinthians 4:18). The Bible tells us about a giant Philistine named Goliath, who caused great terror to God's people. God's promises and blessings for His people Israel were being blocked because they had forgotten what God had promised them. Instead of trusting in God, they preferred to depend more on their own strength against that menacing giant. God's purposes were paralyzed by a nine-foot giant. Israel, who had been called and chosen by God, was now being paralyzed by her lack of spiritual focus. The people paid more attention to Goliath's appearance, the breadth of his shoulders, his biceps and triceps. They trembled when they focused on his bronze helmet, his coat of mail that weighed 125 pounds, and the bronze greaves that covered his legs. The bronze javelin he carried between his shoulders weighed 15 pounds. His shield weighed so much that a man (his shield bearer) carried it in front of him. When David heard that God's troops were being defied, he was not interested in discovering the impressive résumé of the one who was threatening God's people. He knew that God's promises were far more powerful than the threats of his opponent. This strength and conviction came from his relationship with God. He was a young man who had an intimate relationship with the living God. As a result, God honored His Word the moment David needed Him to back it up. The young man not only defied the giant, but also caused a supernatural response when he committed his battle to God: "This day the LORD will hand you over to me, and I'll strike you down."

It is important not to forget that when we exercise our faith, the storms and winds that are sent our way to destroy us are really useful instruments that help to launch us into our destiny. "And we know that all things work together for good to those who love God, to those who are the called according to His purpose" (Romans 8:28). Do you love God? Have you been called by Him? Does God have a purpose for you? If your answer to one of these questions is in the affirmative, I congratulate you, because every threat thrown at you will work in your favor.

Be encouraged and trust in what God has promised you. Your promise may be spiritual or material. Don't lose heart nor miss the help God intends for you; be encouraged, and God will respond in His designated time. Even though the vessel that must carry you to the place God has promised seems to be breaking apart into pieces, take heart! God has said that even if the vessel suffers loss, you and your loved ones will be protected until you reach the destiny He has for you. Do not focus too much on temporal losses; fix your eyes on eternal gains.

In Matthew 13:24–30, we read what Jesus said about the parable of the wheat and the tares:

> Another parable He put forth to them, saying: "The kingdom of heaven is like a man who sowed good seed in his field; but while men slept, his enemy came and sowed tares among the wheat and went his way. But when the grain had sprouted and produced a crop, then the tares also appeared. So the servants of the owner came and said to him, 'Sir, did you not sow good seed in your field? How then does it have tares?' He said to them, 'An enemy has done this.' The servants said to him, 'Do you want us then to go and gather them up?' But he said, 'No, lest while you gather up the tares you also uproot the wheat with them. Let both grow together until the harvest.'"

At times we pray asking God to pull out the negative from our lives and undo every bad situation, tragedy, sickness, or disaster. When we don't see the desired answer to our prayers, we question God. Many have rebelled because they do not understand why the problems (tares) grew together with the blessings (wheat).

Our human mind can only interpret the natural. For this reason, the Bible says: "The carnal mind cannot understand

God." In Psalm 73, the psalmist is confused about not seeing the "wheat" of His faithfulness and instead only notices the "tares" of the wicked. He writes: "But as for me, my feet had almost stumbled; my steps had nearly slipped. For I was envious of the boastful, when I saw the prosperity of the wicked" (v. 2).

The tares are always necessary so that the wheat grows. Pain and suffering fertilize our destiny. How could we ever be victorious without conflicts? Opposing winds are imperative to achieving our goal and fulfilling our destiny.

Joseph had to suffer in order to arrive at his final destiny. His brother's betrayal, the plot of Potiphar's wife, and years in prison served as an incubator for his evolving destiny. According to Genesis 45:5, everything was part of God's plan.

The treatment David received from his brothers helped prepare his character and formed his courage and tenacity. Years of being ignored by his father Jesse, and the object of mockery by his older brother Eliab, served as a training ground for him to step up to the boxing ring to confront the oppressor Goliath. Hebrews 5:7–8 says, "[And Christ] who, in the days of His flesh, when He had offered up prayers and supplications, with vehement cries and tears to Him who was able to save Him from death, and was heard because of His godly fear, though He was a Son, yet He learned obedience by the things which He suffered."

Even Jesus had to experience pain, sufferings, and anguishes in order to learn to be obedient. I am convinced that God the Father used Jesus' disciples to develop patience and obedience during the days of His humanity. And even though

He was the Son of God, while He lived as a human being, He had to deal with the "tares" of life.

In the same way, God allows winds and storms to perfect us. My peace is in knowing that if I obey His Word and honor Him with my life, no matter how bad the situation is, He will allow to come into my life whatever He sees I need, in order to produce in me something that "normal situations" could never bring about. Romans 8:28 encourages us when it says that "And we know that all things work together for good to those who love God, to those who are the called according to His purpose."

Discussion Questions for Chapter 2

1. Can you write down a promise made about your life?
2. What are some of the storms that have arisen to dim the destiny God has for you?
3. In what way can you begin to fight in order to see that promise become a reality?
4. What are some of the seeds the enemy has sown in the ground of your heart?
5. After having read chapter 2, what is your concept of "tares"?
6. In what areas can you thank God even for the negative?
7. How do you see the "tares" helping the "wheat" to grow?
8. Explain in what areas your excitement has grown regarding fulfilling your purpose?

MARK VEGA
JAN. 9, 1970 –

Chapter 3

Do You Know How to Light a Fire?

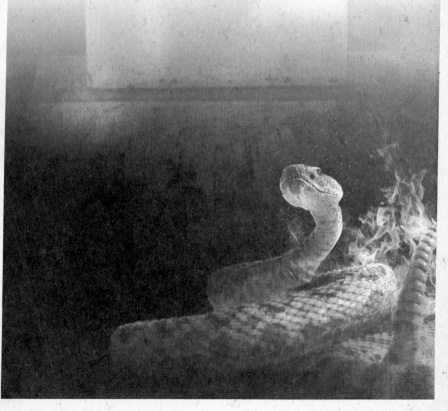

> *But when Paul had gathered a bundle of sticks and laid them*
> *on the fire . . .* (Acts 28:3)

Already saved and living his faith fully, Paul finds himself in a dilemma. Having suffered the ravages of a shipwreck, he is experiencing a rainy and cold night. He looks for sticks to start a fire. He needs to warm himself up so he doesn't become ill and die. Dry sticks in a storm? What was Paul thinking when he began to look for dry sticks in the rain? Pastor Rod Parsley says: "The proof of desire is in pursuit." Paul understood that in order to survive that storm without getting sick and possibly dying, he had to find dry sticks.

Interestingly, Paul knew that God would come to his aid and provide him with what he needed. Nevertheless, we don't see him asking God to send fire from heaven as it happened in the case of Elijah. It is good to know that God takes care of us, but He is not going to do for us what we can do for ourselves. God's sovereignty and omnipotence are not a license for us not to have to work and do our part.

All of God's promises require maintenance. God gives them to you and provides you with the resources to carry them out, but their fulfillment depends on how you react in the process. A photograph is developed in a dark room. The darker the room, the clearer the developing process. But if a ray of light penetrates the room during the developing process, the whole process is destroyed. God wants us to show Him that even in the dark we will trust His Word. No matter how dark the process is, we will never turn aside from the goal. The widow of Zarephath only had a handful of wheat and a little oil, but after following the prophet's instructions, she was able to benefit from a miracle: there was an ongoing provision of wheat and oil according to her faith in the word given by the prophet (see 1 Kings 17:13). No matter what your situation, God always has sufficient ingredients to "cook" a miracle. For Noah, it was wood and pegs (faith); for Moses, it was a staff (trust); for David, it was his harp and sling (bravery); for Samson, it was the jaw of an ass (security); for Gideon, it was a small group of three hundred men (fierceness); for Jesus, it was five loaves of bread and two fish (compassion).

If Paul had let himself be governed by his common sense, the storm would have discouraged him. And trying to find dry sticks in that moment would have seemed like a total impossibility. Paul seriously looked for dry wood. He earnestly walked along the beach looking for wood that he would need to start a fire that would help him survive in that inclement weather.

God always arranges to have the necessary components available in order to carry out His plan in us. As improbable as your specific situation may look, there is a miracle that perhaps is hidden for the moment. Perhaps the miracle is suspended like a pendulum, subject to our faith and determination. God's promises do not depend on economic, political, or family circumstances. If God has given you a word, do not stop believing it. Although everything may appear the opposite, keep fighting and believing in that promise.

Maybe life seems like it wants to give you everything that

is contrary to what God has promised you, but do not faint. The health of your home, marriage, family, ministry, and career does not depend on what happens to you in your daily life; rather it depends on your faith. If you can believe it, you will see it happen. You have to continue fighting to attain the miracle you're looking for, the healing you need, the complete freedom so desired, whether it be for yourself or for a loved one.

If Paul had given up, sickness would have attacked him fiercely, destroying every opportunity to be healed. The effects of pneumonia and other infections are the common results after a storm like this. I can picture Paul with a bad cough brought on by being exposed to a cold and rainy night. But he rejects the fatigue and refuses to surrender to external influences. I'm sure that at some point he was about to give up and die, but at that exact moment it's possible he remembered the word God had given him before leaving on that trip: ". . . since not a hair will fall from the head of any of you" (Acts 27:34).

Paul refuses to give up; instead, he fights with all his strength until he finds the dry sticks he is looking for.

If you want to be a conqueror, you will have to dig deep into your situation to find your "dry sticks." Let me warn you beforehand: you will not find them at the beginning of your search, but do not give up, take courage, keep digging, even though you are overcome with fatigue. I promise that you will soon reach what God has put in your path, the necessary resources to give you intense heat, energy, and light to guide you on to your destiny.

During an evangelistic tour that my wife and I made in

1998 through Cuba, we found ourselves giving some marital conferences. In the corner of the classroom during one meeting sat a couple that had decided to succumb to the problematic situation that was destroying their marriage. The husband had the letter of divorce in his hand; for two years they had not found the "dry sticks" in the storm. Another couple had invited them to church; as a last attempt they decided to come. In that conference they were able to find the "dry sticks" they needed to keep their marriage intact. That afternoon, God intervened on behalf of that couple. They were able to forgive each other, and they found marital reconciliation and God's forgiveness. I know people who have been on the edge of destruction, but by their determination they were able to find the "dry sticks," and today they are enjoying again a new warmth from God. Perhaps your doctor has diagnosed you with a life-threatening sickness; declare your situation to God. Hide that handkerchief you use when you cry; it's time to "dig deep." Your healing is at hand. Ask God for guidance and wisdom, and He will tell you where to dig deep. "Trust in the LORD with all your heart, and lean not on your own understanding" (Proverbs 3:5). Just as God provided the impossible for Paul—the dry sticks in a hurricane—He will do the impossible for you as well.

Everything is possible for him who believes!

The fire represents the presence of the Lord, which is essential in our lives. The warmth of the Holy Spirit fights off sicknesses and infections that at times are caused by the storms of life. The presence of God in us means an intimate relationship with Him. Paul realized that it was a priority to look for dry sticks to build a fire. Notice that he doesn't ask for help from anyone. When you decide to build a spiritual fire in your life, you cannot depend on others. You have to know how to establish an intimate relationship with God. Primarily, God gives us a church where we can persevere in the faith, a pastor who shepherds us, and brothers and sisters with whom we can have fellowship, but we must depend totally and absolutely on our God.

You cannot rely just on Sundays or religious events. In regard to the church, the Bible says, "and the gates of Hades shall not prevail against it" (Matthew 16:18). It is possible to have a continual personal revival in our lives.

Paul and Silas began a "fire" in the jail where they were prisoners. They did not wait until they left to begin rejoicing and praising God. While they were still held as prisoners, they sang and worshipped Him. With their voices they began to pile "dry sticks" onto the fire. Picture them: they were in the depths of the jail where for sure there were foul odors, filth, and even human waste. There, in the lowest part of the dungeon, a place of great mental and physical anguish, it was dark and cold. Undoubtedly, you could hear the shouts, the curses, and the torture the prisoners suffered. It was an environment laden with terrible oppression and great loneliness. Nevertheless, Paul and Silas had a relationship so intimate with God that even with their feet in clamps, they began to pray and sing hymns to God with such force that suddenly an earthquake occurred that shook the jail, causing the doors to open and the chains to fall off their hands.

There is a big difference between a thermometer and a thermostat. A thermometer is passive and only reflects the environment. Although a room is uncomfortable, the thermometer cannot produce any change. It can only measure the atmosphere. There are people who have the mentality of a thermometer. They are always reflecting the problems that surround them and the discomfort of their atmosphere (situation); they are controlled by their surroundings. When they are surrounded by happiness, they smile, but when they are surrounded by bitterness and problems, they always wear a sad and worried face.

A thermostat is different in function. It not only recognizes its environment, but it also can bring about change to its surroundings. Instead of being passive, the thermostat is aggressive. It refuses to be controlled by the temperature, rather it changes the environment by influencing the temperature. God wants you to change your situation. Salt produces thirst, but it also serves to season and preserve food. Light rebukes and destroys darkness, and brings clarity to a room, illuminating everything. Perhaps your situation is dense darkness and coldness, but even if it is, don't let your circumstances determine your faith and praise. Open your mouth, clap your hands, and glorify God because what is happening inside you is more powerful than what is happening around you. Hallelujah!

I challenge you to begin a "fire" in your home, in your church, in your school, or in your ministry. Wherever it is, seek God's presence. Praise Him, worship Him, call out to Him, pray, sing hymns to Him. His presence is indispensable and necessary for your life. Take a few minutes now and prepare a place to invite God's presence.

The key to a true experience in Christ is to seek Him while He can be found. His Word says: "Draw near to God and He will draw near to you" (James 4:8). Your intense seeking for God's presence is explosive and will cause a fire in your spirit. I promise that if you make a great effort to light a fire for God in your life, you will be ablaze with the glory of God: "Therefore I remind you to stir up the gift of God which is in you" (2 Timothy 1:6).

The process for spiritual growth in us is to endure the hard times and depend totally on the Lord. "Many are the afflictions of the righteous, but the Lord delivers him out of them all." (Psalm 34:19). "A broken and a contrite heart—These, O God, You will not despise" (Psalm 51:17). Our calling out to God moves Him: "Call to Me, and I will answer you" (Jeremiah 33:3), and He will do what is necessary to help you in your need.

Paul understood that this fire was crucial for surviving the darkness of the night and for reaching his destiny. Paul was most likely facing all the necessary elements for causing pneumonia or some other sickness.

Do you know how to start a fire? Remember that this kind of fire is not a luxury, but rather a necessity to survive and dispel the sicknesses and dangers that are approaching. Satan will do everything possible to keep you stuck in spiritual coldness. Do not faint. Keep looking for dry wood. If you want the fire to last, you must continuously find dry wood.

The Old Testament tells us the place where the burnt of-fering was made. There, the animal was tied to the wood. The quality of the wood determined the time it would take to con-sume the sacrifice. Good wood was used to keep the fire burn-ing. It required a lot of work to look for and find good dry wood. At times we are satisfied with the heat from "tempo-rary" flames, and we do not recognize the benefit of continu-ing the search for "good wood." The length of the fire depends on our effort to intensify the flames with dry wood. One mo-ment of carelessness and the fire can go out.

Just because you have some areas on fire in your life does not mean you have reached your goals. All of us have experi-enced moments of victory or of sporadic "flames" when we went to church or attended a religious event. Many times we believe we have fulfilled that which was required of us, and now we can rest because we have succeeded in easing our conscience. We entertain ourselves with the idea that we don't have to pray, go to church regularly, or consecrate ourselves more because of the "fire" from the past. It is very easy to live on the successes and glories of the past. But when we finally re-alize that, it's too late. The only thing we're left with from that fire are cold ashes. I want to emphasize that it's not just enough to make a fire; but you also have to keep it going. Paul counsels Timothy: "Rekindle the fire that is in you." In other words, do not let it go out. Do not let the wood run out, be-cause the fire needs to keep burning. "And the fire on the altar shall be kept burning on it; it shall not be put out. And the priest shall burn wood on it every morning, and lay the burnt offering in order on it; and he shall burn on it the fat of the peace offerings. A fire shall always be burning on the altar; it shall never go out" (Leviticus 6:12–13). It was crucial that the priest keep the altar burning with the fire required by God. When God informed Moses about the importance of the fire on the altar, He gave him meticulous details that he required from the priest. He instructed Moses on how to build an altar of incense, foreshadowing it with what would be expected of believers in the future that was to come.

The altar is the believer's heart, and the wood represents everything that can be burnt. The more sacrificial your offering, the more pleasing it will be to God; and the more pleasing it is to God, the more it will burn. All those things that cost you in surrendering to God voluntarily will always be burnable. That which can be burnt up are the things that hurt when you surrender them to God. Everything you are going to sacrifice has to be tied to the wood. The more expensive it is, the more it will burn before God. Abraham tied Isaac up to sacrifice him. The valuable, pleasing, and burnable sacrifices have to be tied up. Six thousand years would have to go by before Paul gave similar instructions to Timothy when he said: "Rekindle the fire (the gift) that is in you."

To please God, Aaron and his sons had to burn the fat in the mornings. The pieces of fat were a symbol for sin. Everything that is not pleasing to God has to be burned in order to attain the favor and mercy of Jehovah. Why couldn't they wait until the afternoon or the night to make this offering? Because the morning represents priority and consecration.

Total separation. God is pleased when we give Him priority and give precedence to holiness, and do not postpone removing harmful and sinful things from our lives. Our character, integrity, and personal life must have no "fat," or sin. If sin is not exposed to the flames, it will defile the altar and displease God.

Though severe, these rules were for the people's benefit. Many pastors, in order to not offend the brethren, have completely eliminated the subject of sin. They have ostentatious buildings, large congregations, but the "fat" is thriving too.

Now, pause and evaluate your own altar. Is the fire burning, or is there an abundance of "fat"? The Bible tells us: "Let us lay aside every weight, and the sin which so easily ensnares us" (Hebrew 12:1). Dear reader, you have the power to change your situation right now. The Bible also reminds us that "where sin abounded, grace abounded much more" (Romans 5:20). If you're guilty of letting the "fat" put out the flame of your altar, remember that God is willing to restore the fire. Simply ask sincerely and prepare yourself, because your life will change forever. Even though repentance has a negative connotation, God has intended it as a means of forgiveness, peace, and restoration. Don't procrastinate. "Call to Me, and I will answer you, and show you great and mighty things, which you do not know" (Jeremiah 33:3). In doing so, you will find rest for your life. Now I want to ask you a personal question. Are you keeping the fire in your life burning high or low, or has it gone out? Whatever the case, I want to give you a word of encouragement. Tell the Lord right now that you're not satisfied with the degree of your fire. Tell Him: "God, by the Holy Spirit, give me more of Your presence, more of Your fire, more of Your passion." Throw wood on the fire with your praise and worship. Begin to live the kind of life that produces the continual presence of the Lord in you. In order to keep the fire burning, you have to leave mediocrity behind. You have to leave the traditional crowd and enter into a new dimension, where you are not ashamed of the gospel because it is the power of God.

If you become ashamed, instead of receiving power, you will experience spiritual weakness. A weak believer is ineffective in the Kingdom of God, because the devil will then tend to interfere in all of the areas of your life: the spiritual, emotional, and physical.

Escape from the trap of worrying about the opinions of other people. Forget what they think of you and begin to look for the good "wood" to light the fire that will consume your life completely.

Discussion Questions for Chapter 3

1. What does the fulfillment of God's promise in our lives depend on?
2. What is needed in order to be an overcomer?
3. What should we do with the dry "sticks"?
4. Do you prefer to be a thermometer or a thermostat?
5. How will you start a fire in your life?
6. What kind of wood are you throwing on your fire?

7. How burnable is your offering?

8. What do you have to do in order to keep your fire burning?

MARK VEGA
JAN. 9, 1970 –

Chapter 4

Beware of the Snake!

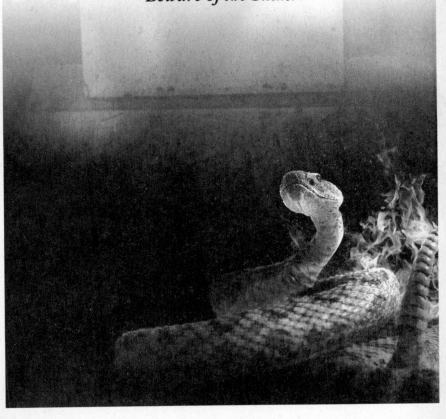

. . . a viper came out because of the heat, and fastened on his
hand. So when the natives saw the creature hanging from his
hand, they said to one another, "No doubt this man is a mur-
derer, whom, though he has escaped the sea, yet justice does not
allow to live." (Acts 28:3b–4)

If you feel satisfied with your spiritual life, this chapter is not for you, but if you are not afraid to stir up the evil one, keep reading. When Paul begins to warm himself by the fire, suddenly a viper attacks him. Notice that the viper is stirred by the *heat*.

While he was surrounded by the cold and darkness, the viper was comfortable. The viper is a cold-blooded animal. It is relaxed and tranquil in that environment. The temptation to confuse stagnation with stability exists. If we don't define these concepts well, we are going to think that we are free of these kinds of attacks, and we'll believe we are living a high level of spirituality. As long as you are not a threat to Satan's kingdom, the demons will have no problem with you. But when you recognize that you have to abandon religiosity in your life in order to enter into an intimacy with God, then that is when you will begin to experience attacks. The warmth and presence of the Holy Spirit will make the diabolic forces uncomfortable. When they feel that heat, they will become furious. As long as we are comfortable, living cold and/or mediocre lives, the enemy will have no problem with us.

An attack comes in distinct ways: *spiritually,* you will experience attacks on your faith, your hope, your prayer life, your biblical beliefs, your personal witness and your relationships with your brothers and sisters; *emotionally,* you will experience negative thoughts, fears, anxiety, tensions, and depression; *physically,* sicknesses, neurological problems, appetite loss, ulcers, insomnia, and abnormal tiredness might appear.

The viper attacks with a specific plan because his ultimate goal is to kill you. This attack is not normal; it is intense and spontaneous. It generally occurs when you determine to go on to the next level with God, seeking Him with greater tenacity; that is when you will discover the enemy's fangs. The devil is predictable. When you enter into a more intimate relationship with God, breaking every barrier of religiosity, aloofness and laziness, the enemy will certainly assign his agents (demons) to hinder your walk and try to extinguish your fire for God. The viper thinks that if he can kill you spiritually, emotionally, or physically, he will also be able to wipe out and destroy God's purposes in your life.

We are told in Matthew 4 that when Jesus had finished his fast, Satan was waiting for Him with three different temptations. When a believer stops being in God's presence, the enemy is waiting to tempt him. "God is faithful, who will not allow you to be tempted beyond what you are able, but with the temptation will also make the way of escape, that you may be able to bear it" (1 Corinthians 10:13). It is not until one has experienced great victories in their life that the most severe attacks come. In 1 Kings 18, God answered Elijah with fire to burn up the sacrifice, and the prophet killed the 450 prophets of Baal. When the news spread, Jezebel and Ahab threatened to kill him. Elijah, instead of confronting both of them with the assurance of God having just backed him up with fire from heaven, begins to run away terrorized, and he goes into the desert to hide under a juniper tree. It is possible that the blood of the prophets that he had just killed was still on his clothes, as evidence that God was on his side, but it appears that he wants to make a final decision solely based on a temporary situation.

By not confronting the viper, many of us have hidden in caves and under trees. God does not want us to run, but rather, to submit to Him and resist the devil so that he flees (see James 4:2).

Remember, when you say, "Yes, Lord, I am here, whatever you want. I am willing to serve you with my life," a viper waits for you not far away, ready to sink his fangs into you. But always remember that greater is He who is in you, than he who is against you.

Get That Snake Off Me!

With a lot of subtlety, the viper comes out of the leaves without anyone noticing it. How does he do it? Because he blends in with his surroundings. He meticulously studies his victim before attacking. "Be sober, be vigilant; because your adversary the devil walks about like a roaring lion, seeking whom he may devour" (1 Peter 5:8). As soon as he sees his opportunity, the viper slithers toward his victim to attack him. Without his intentions being detected, he fixes his eyes on the target to destroy him. "The thief does not come except to steal, and to kill, and to destroy" (John 10:10).

If we knew how vulnerable we were, our devotion and

fervor would intensify even more. Your life can change in an instant. At times, we drop our guard because we believe we are invulnerable. Job's life went from blessing to blessing because God considered him a faithful servant. And in one instant, he lost his children, cattle, earnings, friends, and even his wife's support. All his earthy possessions came crashing down.

There are preachers who lose their voice without warning. Suddenly, car accidents, sicknesses, and catastrophes drastically change the lives of millions. There are people who were enjoying a secure, prosperous financial life, but because of a sickness that required hospitalization, in the blink of an eye, they ended up in bankruptcy.

Satan is devoted to launching spontaneous attacks that no one expects, causing great damage. In the world of boxing they say that the most effective blow is the one the opponent is not expecting.

Suddenly, when he is close enough, the viper latches onto Paul's hand. He feels the fangs penetrating his flesh and receives a dose of venom that causes him excruciating pain. The people who are near when he is bit hear him cry out and see the viper hanging from his hand. They refuse to offer him help. Perhaps Paul was hoping Luke would give him first aid, or one of his friends in the ministry would pray for him, or that someone would grab the viper by the neck and kill it. But nothing happened. What did occur was they began to accuse and condemn him.

Many of those who have persevered in the faith have gone astray because no one helped them in their time of need. The devil has deceived them, causing them to doubt and causing uncertainty in their minds. He has whispered: "No one loves you. Nobody cares about your need." He lies to them, making them believe that their lives have no value, or that they aren't important.

The enemy frequently launches these snares at you immediately after you are attacked. It is true that the enemy knows when someone is the most vulnerable. Paul now finds himself going through a time of emotional uncertainty. There's no doubt that the devil is whispering to him: "Where is your help? Where is the God you serve, who lets his servant die in disgrace in front of everyone?" I can picture the devil laughing at Paul and celebrating because of the difficult situation in which Paul finds himself. Undoubtedly, Paul is feeling the depression of loneliness while the five-pound viper, whose bite is fatal, is hanging from his hand.

Sometimes, when we are going through a time of extreme depression, the fact that no one reaches out to offer help wounds us more than the attack itself. The pain caused by rejection penetrates deep into the soul, where only God can heal. Paul raises his eyes and looks around. He sees none of his friends doing anything to help him. No one is doing anything to free him from that horrendous experience. And that was just the least of what happened, listen to what the people then begin to say: "This man is a murderer. It's okay that this happened to him. He brought it on himself." That sounds like a death sentence to Paul.

Have you ever gone through a bad experience believing

that someone was going to help you, but instead of offering you a hand to help you, they have judged you? Have you ever experienced being the subject of intense gossip, all the while knowing full well that you were innocent? Have you been faithful to God, are you a good Christian, do you have a good testimony, are you a good father, a good mother, a model youth, an excellent worker, a minister of integrity, but instead of being praised, they insult you?

Jesus sympathized with Paul, and He sympathizes with you. The Son of God, who was innocent, never hurt anyone; nevertheless, he was the object of many abuses. His enemies, who wanted to see him dead, mocked Him and judged Him unfairly. He never defended himself nor opened His mouth. He knew that God would come to His defense at the right time.

In the same way, Paul neither defends nor justifies himself. Instead, he prefers God to be his witness, choosing rather to depend totally on the power of the Holy Spirit.

Paul's example should serve to show us that when we go through times of criticism, gossip, and accusations, we should remember that Jesus is always interceding for us. He is our lawyer; he pleads our case and defends us.

If you find yourself defenseless and going through moments when no one is running to your defense when you most need support, trust in the Lord and in the power of His Word. God will help you, no matter what your need is. Don't rush to defend yourself. Allow the Holy Spirit to do that for you. I encourage you to trust in Christ and in His Word. If you are faithful to Him, you will see help come soon. The favor and grace of the Lord are essential for us. It is true that thousands of people have turned aside from their faith, looking for a solution to their problems in their own power. Their wounds have caused them much pain, mostly because of not being aware of the faithfulness and justice of God. Consequently, their situation has gotten worse. Don't take vengeance, even when you believe you have the right to do it. Let God be the One who defends you.

Satan wants to blind us to God's faithfulness, grace, and favor. If we acknowledge that God is always on our side, watching and taking care of us, He will give us peace and rest in the middle of the storm. Paul teaches us the importance of being guided by the Spirit and not by the flesh. It says in Galatians 5:17: "For the flesh lusts against the Spirit, and the Spirit against the flesh; and these are contrary to one another, so that you do not do the things that you wish."

The devil wants to use your flesh to bring misery and anxiety into your life. Many people, when they don't see a way out, drown in their own desperation. These same people make the terrible mistake of making bad decisions even for small problems. They act impulsively when they don't see a way out. It is sad when people with brilliant futures decide to end their life trying to escape anguish and pain. I'm sure Paul's carnal nature was telling him: "You are going to die, and nobody will care. God's promises are never going to be fulfilled in your life." But, on the other hand, his spirit was telling him: "You can do all things through Christ who strengthens you." As believers, we have to discipline our flesh to learn to submit to the Spirit. Years before, Paul himself wrote to the Philippians: "Finally, brethren, whatever things are true, whatever things are noble, whatever things are just, whatever things are pure, whatever things are lovely, whatever things are of good report, if there is any virtue and if there is anything praiseworthy— meditate on these things" (Philippians 4:8). Jesus said: "the flesh is weak, but the spirit is willing."

We must take captive every thought to make it obedient to Christ. Like Paul, we must refuse to give up and instead fight the good fight of faith. Paul avoids death and defeat by focusing, concentrating, and ignoring the enemy's threats. The most surprising thing is that the inhabitants from the island are the ones who initiate the verbal attack against Paul when they see the viper hanging from his hand. They believe that the serpent was an indication of the kind of person Paul was. There are those who believe that an honest and pure believer cannot be attacked by the devil. The Bible tells us about men and women whom God used mightily, but they went through the crucible of affliction and injustice. Our spiritual position does not exempt us from Satan's attacks or problems. It is a fact that the more we seek the Lord's presence, the more we are going to stir up Satan's kingdom. We will never see someone attacking a vagabond, but we have seen assassinations of well-known politicians who have made a difference in their country. When we walk uprightly and make a difference, this will incite attacks and storms in our lives. The Bible tells us about Joseph, who was sold as a slave. He was treated unfairly, locked up in a jail, and suffered in many other ways for being a righteous man. In the same manner, Job lost everything just for being a righteous man before God. Being honest, righteous, and noble has its price. Are you willing to pay the price?

If Joseph had let himself be seduced by Potiphar's wife, he would not have gone through so many difficulties. But because he fled from her sexual advances, he had to spend seven years in jail; however, in the end he was exalted. Even though he was sold into slavery by his brothers, he recognized God's hand moving in his life. Later on, he tells his brothers, who had sold him: "But now, do not therefore be grieved or angry with yourselves because you sold me here; for God sent me before you to preserve life" When Joseph's brothers come to Egypt to buy wheat, Joseph ponders over all his past experiences and ends up saying: "God sent me." You may find yourself reading this book, and you still do not understand why you have been the victim of so many negative things. Let me encourage you by saying: "God sent you." He has had control and currently has control of each situation in your life. The sovereignty of God is our peace. I have never taken an antidepressant or a "relaxer" to calm my nerves. When I think about God's sovereignty, I can lay my head on His sovereign lap and know that He will embrace me because He loves me, and everything is going to be fine because He has control over everything: ". . . casting all your care upon Him, for He cares for you" (1 Peter 5:7).

Shake Yourself

With intense pain in his soul and his body, Paul violently

shakes the viper. At some point we will have to decide what we are going to do with the viper. We have two options: we can treat it with a lot of respect and fear, asking it to let go of us and leave, or we can kill it. At times fear can hinder us and keep us from operating at our maximum capacity. We make the enemy and his attacks greater than what they really are. We yield to the attacker simply because we are terrified of a confrontation. We avoid that confrontation at all costs. Thousands of people have been sexually abused by a family member or an acquaintance, and because of the fear, shame, and even feelings of guilt, they prefer to suffer silently in torment for the rest of their lives. Because of that they choose to sacrifice themselves, and they continue living a nightmare instead of allowing God to set them free. The devil lies to them, telling them that if they open their mouths to free themselves from the viper, they are going to suffer severe repercussions. These threats of Satan have trapped multitudes of people in many places in the world and even within our churches. There are believers who on the outside seem to be living lives of freedom and seem to be enjoying a religious life, but inwardly, they are still living behind the bars of their terrifying experiences. Freedom cannot be received passively. If you're only living and tolerating your situation, you will never confront it. You are only experiencing what you have allowed to come into your life.

The only way we are going to receive deliverance is by confessing our wounds and their pain, and then allowing God to heal us. If we consider ourselves victims or sinners, 1 John 1:9 tells us: "If we confess our sins, He is faithful and just to forgive us our sins." The pain comes in different degrees and affects different areas in a person's life. We are susceptible spiritually, physically, emotionally, in our marriage and ministry, but the medicine is still the same: a close relationship with our God. The other option we have is to shake off the viper into the fire and kill it, which signifies handing our pain, traumas, and bad experiences over to God. Paul decides to shake off the viper into the fire. It is important for us not to believe that just because we attend a church everything is going to be fine. We tend to believe that if we turn over our problems to the pastor, or one of the more mature brothers or sisters in the faith, or to the evangelist, everything is going to be taken care of. The viper doesn't die unless it is thrown into the fire. We must take the initiative of removing every mental, emotional, and spiritual obstacle in God's presence.

Let's Pray

Father, I take control of my life in the name of Jesus. I shake off this viper that has fastened itself to me, that has clung to my life to kill me. By the power of the Holy Spirit, I loose myself from the pain, the abuse, and the fear. Even though nobody has been able to help me, I surrender my life to you, and I also renounce everything that has kept me bound to the past. In the powerful name of Jesus Christ . . . Amen.

As long as the fire is still lit, you can be sure that the snake will not show back up in your life. Shaking means movement. There should be movement and action in your spiritual life. If Paul had remained still, the viper would have killed him.

There's danger when a person is inactive in their faith. The devil's plan is to immobilize you to the point that you are not alert to the things of the Lord. When you get up in the morning with no desire to live, depression and anguish come and try to build a nest in your heart.

We must keep moving forward in the Lord. Let us continue to pray daily, participating regularly in the activities of the church, and using our gifts, talents, and abilities given by God. Maintain a strong discipline in order to study and apply God's Word on a consistent basis.

Just because the viper dies doesn't mean that its effects died. The viper hanging from Paul's hand has been shaken into the fire. The viper is dead. But I must warn you, however, not to be quick to celebrate. It's true the viper is dead, but the venom stayed in Paul's body. At times we believe that just because the attack ceases, the effects of the attack die. Just because we don't have contact with the assailant, because he died or moved to another city, we believe we can rest, and everything will return to normal. It's amazing that there are people who are not careful about their lives just because they see that the attack has stopped. When we go for a doctor's appointment for some infection, the doctor prescribes us a medication. And when we leave his office, he stresses the importance of taking or applying the medicine before the next visit. But if you are like me, we often take the medicine only until we feel better. As soon as we stop feeling the effects of the infection, we forget about the medicine and the instructions the doctor gave us. Perhaps this example makes us laugh, but the truth is that we cannot adopt the same attitude with our spiritual life. Every attack has its effects. Satan also scatters seed, hoping that it will produce fruit in due time. There are a number of believers who sit in the pews of their churches each week, singing hymns and listening to powerful messages, but they continue to suffer from deep wounds in their souls because of a trauma that occurred years before. That makes for a religious people, but an acrimonious one. They are victims of resentment, pain, and bitterness, which keep their wounds open. If they do not let God deal with their situation, they will continue to live tormented and inconsistent lives. Though the cause of the dilemma ended years ago, they are still influenced by the side effects that were never healed. The problem is that these infected wounds grow and run rampant through their emotions. While you're reading this book, I'm asking God to reveal these open wounds to you by His Holy Spirit so that you can confess and renounce them once and for all. The hand of God is on your life to heal you.

Forgiveness

Many years can go by before someone is healed of their wounds and their pain. The easiest thing to do is to ignore these harmful emotions and stuff them in the deepest recesses of our memory. The problem with this is that the pain is then often not dealt with until one reaches a more mature age, such as thirty, forty, or fifty. When the person finally realizes it, decades of their life have been robbed from them. The past infects the present and destroys the future. When you decide to forgive those responsible for your pain, you will no longer be a prisoner to them. Anger is like an umbilical cord that keeps you connected to your past. As long as you hold on to your anger, you will remain bound to the one who abused you, and that same person will control your life. Forgiveness does not necessarily free the person who abused you, but it frees you. Forgiveness is for your own benefit. It's time to stop living in prisons of anger and bitterness that control your mind, emotions, and your future. Forgiveness is the medicine the victim needs. If you do not take care of your past, it will turn into a cancer and infect all of your future.

In Greek, *forgiveness* means "breathe out, exhale" (remove from your system). This does not happen automatically; it's a process. Humanly speaking, it is a very difficult thing, but God will give you the necessary strength to forgive.

It requires a lot of energy to keep hate and bitterness alive. Anger, resentment, and bitterness can still harass you severely, almost as if the abuser were still alive. You will then rehearse the incident all over again. This dilemma, along with what may have been instilled in us when we were kids ("what happens at home stays at home"), is the formula for destroying someone, unless we seek the freedom that is offered in the name of Jesus.

Let's Pray

Father, I come wounded and traumatized. I need your healing balm. I believe the blood of Christ heals me and restores me. I renounce and forgive those who opened the door so that the enemy could use this against me (be specific; name each area). I accept your righteousness, and I am justified by your grace. I will never let this bind me again. Forgive me for not embracing your grace and mercy. The blood of Christ cleanses, forgives, heals, and justifies me in the name of Jesus and by the power of your Word. Thank you, Father. Amen.

Discussion Questions for Chapter 4

1. How can you relate to the terms "stuck" and "stability"?
2. How much heat are you producing?
3. In what way are you a threat to the kingdom of darkness?
4. Why do all these tragedies happen to me?
5. How can you shake off the viper and kill it?
6. How much is your past infecting your future?
7. Name three people you know you need to forgive.
8. Explain the venom in your life and the way it is affecting you.
9. What have you learned about forgiveness?

Chapter 5

The Danger of This Snake Is That It's Venomous

*However, they were expecting that he would swell up or sud-
denly fall down dead.* (Acts 28:6)

An Attack like No Other

When Satan discovers your potential, he launches his attacks to destroy the destiny designed by God for you.
The attacks against certain believers often are an indication of
the calling or destiny God has ordained for them. If you make
a comparison among people, you will notice that not all are
attacked with the same intensity. If you notice, those who are
used of God greatly were those who, beginning with their
childhood, suffered major traumas in their lives. Similarly, you
can ask any ordinary, everyday Christian (mediocre), and they
will tell you that their life has been very normal.

The more threatening Satan sees you, the more attacks he
will launch against you with the purpose of causing you to
pull back and become discouraged in your walk of faith. The
enemy will use different people to make you go astray from
the calling and purpose God put in your life. He may even use
the people who are closest to you to discourage you. The devil
is known for his traps, but he doesn't have anything new to
use. When I see a person come to the feet of Jesus, I always
warn them that attacks will start to come, and they will be like
nothing before. They can expect betrayal from some alleged
friends, hypocrisy and gossip; and the darts from the evil one
will also come to destroy their life, but they must trust in the
power and mercy of our Almighty God.

Paul said that within these jars of clay lies a treasure;

nevertheless, in order for the devil to steal this treasure from us, he has to break the clay jar. Did you know that for this reason, the devil, from the moment you were born again, has not let one day go by without trying to destroy your faith, peace, and security? The devil does not sleep; he always looks for the way to concoct strategies to strip you of that treasure. It is sad that thousands of people have taken their eyes off God's eternal purposes and have instead focused on these temporary attacks, thus staying distracted and out of the race to win the eternal prize.

Job did not go through the fire coincidently. He was a man of integrity. Did you know there's a price to pay for being honest, upright, and living a consecrated life in order to honor God? There will come moments when you will ask yourself: "Will it be worth it to serve God? Is it worth it to endure the pain, the process of being fashioned into His likeness like the clay in the potter's hand?" But in the depths of your spirit, there will be a resounding affirmation: "Yes, it's worth it, my Lord Jesus!" Nothing can be compared to the price that Christ paid for us on the cross of Calvary, taking our curse and carrying on Himself our sins, sicknesses, and mankind's trespasses there on the cross, where He finally declared with a loud voice: "It is finished!" In the same way that Jesus fought and battled, we also should do the same until we hear: "Well done, good and faithful servant; you were faithful over a few things, I will make you ruler over many things. Enter into the joy of your lord" (Matthew 25:21).

Paul is going through a transition in his spiritual life. God has plans, purposes, and assignments He has prepared for him. Satan recognizes that he cannot allow Paul to continue to live because he will cause much damage and threat to his demonic kingdom. Paul is a man known by all the demons of hell. I can visualize pictures of Paul hanging in all the hallways of hell with captions such as: "Most Wanted." Acts 19:15 tells us that one demon declared: "Jesus I know, and Paul I know; but who are you?" While Paul's name reverberates throughout hell's corridors, the demons vote to seek him out and destroy him. At times, being exempt from satanic attacks does not necessarily mean that we are spiritually well. I do not want to be dogmatic, but I believe that sometimes the absence of attacks is indicative of the fact that we are not doing enough to be a threat to the kingdom of darkness. Why would the devil waste his demonic forces on someone who is not a threat to the satanic kingdom? He has his gaze on those who are causing a revolution and reclaiming lost ground from the kingdom of darkness.

In basketball, each team that competes is made up of five players. At times a coach may put two of his players to guard the other team's best player. Why? Because he is the best player, one who represents such a danger that he can cause them a defeat. Satan uses the same tactic with the most dangerous believers. At times, he uses a legion of demons to try to diminish the damage caused to his army. For that reason, when we are a spiritual threat, Satan does everything he can to end our life. But thanks to God, greater is He who is in us than he who is against us. It doesn't matter how many legions the devil sends to stop you from attaining the victory; with Christ, we outnumber them.

As a spiritual being, Satan knew that he had to use the most potent weapons in his arsenal to destroy Paul and his ministry of raising up new works and writing two-thirds of the New Testament. In order to kill him, he sent him a viper. Not just an ordinary viper, but a dangerous and venomous one. Satan always uses his most potent weapons to destroy a believer.

With Samson, he did it by using Delilah. Samson used to sleep with prostitutes and with many other women, but Delilah wasn't a woman like the others. She was sent by the princes of the Philistines to uncover the secret of Samson's great strength (Judges 16:5). Even though Delilah had the same appearance as the rest of the other women, she was much more dangerous. Delilah was not sent to distract Samson's focus, nor to make him sin, nor to entertain him, but rather to kill him. While you are reading this book, the devil is planning how to kill you. He prowls around like a roaring lion trying to devour you.

When Paul discovers the viper, notice that it is not like other vipers. Even though it appeared to be like other vipers, this one was different because it carried deadly venom. Many attacks seem to be the same, but they are different. Some are sent to distract, discourage, diminish focus, damage (wound), but there are other attacks that are specifically sent to assassinate. Jesus said it in John 10:10: "The thief does not come except to steal, and to kill, and to destroy."

1. Rob. Minimal damage. Steal, violate, and deceive.

2. Kill. Death means separation. Satan wants to separate you from your faith, from your hope and your love; he wants to cause you spiritual, emotional, and even physical death.

3. Destroy. To cease to exist; to tear down every pillar of faith, to snuff out every breath. That viper wanted to kill Paul and destroy the church. As the key person that God would use to raise up the church, Paul is marked by Satan for destruction. The attacks, then, are indicators of powerful callings.

In the previous chapter, I felt tempted to finish this book when the viper died in the fire. It seemed to me that the biblical story had provided you with a good introduction and made a good exegesis. The death of the serpent would make for a good ending to the story. However, I had to continue writing because the serpent carried venom; because the death of the serpent doesn't mean the effects of the venom die. The moment this viper sinks its fangs into Paul's hand, it is injecting a fatal dose of venom, enough to end his life. The people around him are simply waiting for death to come. The venom has a very bad reputation. Throughout its life, this viper had caused a lot of damage. It had shortened the lives of many people. It is famous for dashing the dreams of multitudes. Paul is marked to be its next victim. No one sees the venom running through Paul's bloodstream. At times, no one sees what is happening in the background of the attack, except God.

By itself, venom is dangerous and lethal. Once injected, its mission is to bring sudden death. The moment someone is bitten, they can feel a hot rush running through their whole body. The venom has four functions to carry out in the body of its victim.

Pain. The first effect is to produce pain. It has been proven that a viper that weighs fifteen pounds can kill a lion that weighs three hundred pounds. Pain spreads throughout the body until it controls everything. Every second that goes by is deadly. The pain takes over every member with the ability to cause permanent damage. Even the mind falls victim to this terrible pain. Thoughts are interrupted and the mind is taken captive. Reasoning becomes distorted, ideas are confused, and one's strength is weakened.

Just as the viper's venom can conquer the king of the jungle; in the same way, a human being can also be controlled by this unbearable pain. Perhaps you are reading this book, and right now you're hiding a venomous pain that entered your system years ago.

The enemy designed a deadly attack, using his venom, to apply to us from the time we are born with the intent of destroying us. Perhaps you have forgotten the time when the viper first attacked you, but when you least expect it, a memory of it comes back. Unconsciously, we go all through life dealing with that "pain." We try to deaden the pain or cover it up temporarily by adopting habits or an unhealthy lifestyle. There are men who were ignored by their father during their childhood who didn't develop a healthy relationship with their father. They now have grown up to be adults and still carry inside themselves the painful remnant of that venom. Even in their own families, with their spouses and children, they can't live a healthy and normal life. Not able to control their actions, they imitate the same behavior of the persons that caused them the pain, and they continue to repeat it and pass it on to others. Wounded people wound others. Pain makes no exception with people. It attacks and controls whoever has been exposed to its deadly venom.

It does not matter what your social level or economic status is—rich, middle class, or poor—pain has a deadly effect that causes emotional ruin in everyone. First it wears you down; then it weakens your strength and your courage until it finally destroys your dreams. Perhaps you're thinking of giving in to something, ignoring the promises God has made to you in His Word. You're perplexed and your dreams, desires, and visions for today only seem like a fantasy. The only clear things that stand out in your mind are the failures of the past. I want to tell you that the prince of darkness is ambushing you to see if you will give up. He knows you have abilities, gifts, and talents that God has given you, and that you will be a serious threat to him here on earth.

Pain has its benefits. It functions as an alarm to warn the body that something isn't working right. The worst you can do is ignore this warning. Doctors say that the majority of heart attacks could have been avoided because there almost always are symptoms that the victim ignored. The majority of them, knowing that they were in danger, refused to go to the hospital for fear of a bad medical diagnosis. Finally, when they decided to go, the damage had already been done. If you are reading this book, I would like you to examine your life right now. If you are ignoring some area in your life and have a pain that no one is aware of, I want you to give it to the Lord right now.

Perhaps you are in a ministry that God called you to and you feel you're not growing as you should or how God promised you would. Seek God earnestly, ask the Holy Spirit to show you what you have to surrender or turn over to Him so that the power of God can flow in a supernatural way.

As I was saying earlier, pain is not only limited to specific people; instead, it intends to do away with every human being. Perhaps you're asking why? And the answer is: Because we are the most beautiful and perfect creation, and we were made in the image and likeness of Almighty God.

If you are a mother, I want you to understand that if you do not surrender that area of your life to the Lord, you will not be able to experience the *zoé* life; that is, the life of God manifested in us. Turn over to the Lord all your worries and pains. He cares for you (1 Peter 5:7). At times, the pain comes because we've been betrayed by some family member, by a friend, or a brother in the faith. Whatever the reason, the result is always the same: unbearable pain.

In our campaigns and evangelism crusades, we are puzzled when we see that more than 70 percent of active believers in the faith come forward to have God get rid of their pain. Sometimes, the pain is from long ago, and it was tolerated and accepted as part of normal feelings. This is exactly what Satan wants: for us to make a bed for the pain so that it becomes a part of our daily life. Once you have become used to living with the pain, its job of letting us know when danger is near will no longer work, and your situation will continue to get worse.

I believe God has allowed me to write this book to serve as a help to provide deliverance to people who are seeking to be completely free. If while you're reading this you feel greater faith and extraordinary encouragement, it's because the Holy Spirit is near you to transform your life right now. If you want to become truly free from this terrible torment, allow me to pray for you. Say the following words out loud:

Let's Pray:
Holy Father, I surrender my life to you right now. I turn this area _____ (be specific) over to you, which has caused me great pain. In the name of Jesus and with the authority of God and His Word, I renounce every hurtful feeling that has controlled my life and my destiny. I break all power of pain, and I apply the blood of Jesus Christ, my Savior, over my life in the name of Jesus. Amen.

Paralysis. As if the pain weren't enough, there is another effect from the venom—paralysis. Paralysis is, in part, a result of pain, but it occurs when the neurological system (nervous system) is damaged. The electrical signals from the brain are sent to the dorsal spine (the center of the nervous system), but what happens is there is a break in the circuit. The neurological system has been damaged. *Webster's Dictionary* defines *paralysis* as "a loss or impediment of voluntary movement." The *Oxford*

Dictionary defines it as "the lack of ability to move normally." Imagine not being able to move yourself with the ability or potential with which you were created. Not being able to use your physical abilities brings with it great frustration. The word *frustration* means "preventing a person from reaching their goal or making them feel useless." Can you identify with that? Jesus said: "The thief does not come except to steal, and to kill, and to destroy" (John 10:10). The devil wants to sidetrack you from your way so that you don't reach the land that flows with milk and honey.

This deadly venom is guaranteed to destroy and kill you. Paul is in line to be the poisonous snake's next victim. I'm sure Paul could have been one more on the list of victims of this animal.

As you continue reading the pages of this book, perhaps you can identify with this chapter and feel a certain connection because you recognize the areas in your life where you are suffering paralysis. Can you remember the good times when you had movement in your extremities? You could stand up on your feet, walk, and move around with ease without having to depend on anyone. As you remember the freedom you used to enjoy, you delight in the memory, but at the same time it causes you bittersweet feelings. When you remember your lack of movement, you feel frustration, despair, and even contempt.

Before the attack came, you used to enjoy a constant and enjoyable communion with God. Being able to talk with Almighty God was not seen as a task, but rather a privilege. The ability to love was so normal that you didn't have to force yourself, but rather love flowed daily in a supernatural way. You loved the people you knew as well as those you didn't know. Reading the Bible was a great delight. The Bible wasn't a foreign book, but a map and guide that you had received personally from God to be a lamp to your feet and a light to your path. Each word filled your heart with plenty of wisdom and faith. Certain words—such as unattainable, incomprehensible or impossible—had no place in your vocabulary. Do you remember the confidence and joy you had, along with the desire to live an abundant life? The desire to please God in everything had no limits. From the moment you opened your eyes until you closed them to sleep, you lived in integrity according to the Word of God. With all that, and in spite of the fact that the world continued on its destructive path with its problems, storms, emotional earthquakes, family and financial destruction, you experienced a deep peace that nobody around you could comprehend.

But now, the venom has caused a paralysis in your life. The fact that you attend church, are part of a ministry team, or have attained a high level of education has not been sufficient to deliver you from your chronic condition. Like many victims who suffer from paralysis, when they recognize their present situation, then remember the past, they are filled with sadness and depression. Their focus changes from fighting against the enemy to fighting against themselves. They fight against self-rejection when they consider their spiritual or emotional condition, and instead of feeling contentment, they feel hate and resentment toward themselves. They blame others for their sad state, and they ignore the one who is really guilty, Satan, the author of their trauma, the one who causes divorce, the one who brings spiritual destruction and paralysis to their life. "We know that we are of God, and the whole world lies *under the sway of* the wicked one" (1 John 5:19).

I Know the Plan, but I Cannot Follow It. I'm Immobilized

Knowing what we have to do and not being able to do anything brings frustration. Paul, when he began his ministry, said the following: "For the good that I will to do, I do not do; but the evil I will not to do, that I practice" (Romans 7:19).

Perhaps you are a person who would like to be a model father, a loving husband, a spiritual priest of your household, upright, and a provider for your family, but paralysis prevents you from doing it. Perhaps you are a woman of destiny and a promising purpose. Your desire is to fulfill all the expectations other people have put on you. You want to be the virtuous woman of Proverbs 31. A mother who takes care of her household, who leads her children by wise example. A wife who can encourage and complement her husband so he can fulfill the purposes of God for which he was called. Do you desire to raise, nurture, and feed your family with the abilities, gifts, and talents God has put in you, but because of the paralysis, you have not been able to achieve it?

Perhaps you are a young person with a brilliant life ahead of you. You have all the resources and abilities to carve out for yourself an outstanding future. You want to invest good things in your generation, and perhaps you feel you are the last hope for someone in your family to excel. The pressures are immense, no one understands your pain and frustration, and there are plenty of people trying to diagnose your paralysis. There is no lack of advice from people with good intentions. However, everything goes on the same. All this torment has caused a lot of internal doubts in your life. The confusion and the insecurity have been the norm in the depths of your soul. The loneliness, sadness, and lack of confidence have ruled your present life. All of this has been at a great cost to your life. Your spiritual strength has been diminished. The Bible speaks about our youth: "Strength is your glory," but you still are weak to the point of immobility due to the paralysis you're suffering from.

I know colleagues who are going through the horrible phase called "paralysis." Many of them are pastors, evangelists, teachers, prophets, and apostles who are having frustrations that come from ministerial paralysis. God has called you, even from childhood, to a specific ministry. You have seen God's hand working. You have experienced the magnitude and faithfulness of the Lord at work. You have had moments of success and indescribable visitations from the Spirit of God, but the venomous snake has sunk its fangs into you and injected that deadly venom into the heart of your ministry. From that time on, you have not been able to function as God intended you to from before the time He created and called you. Your strength has disappeared, you don't trust anyone, and you continue to become discouraged. The vision that God has placed in you today is only a memory. You preach by profession, not by conviction. Prayer has become a traditional ritual. Perhaps your marriage is suffering from the consequences of your paralysis. You realize your family members are also victims of paralysis. This paralysis that has come upon them is worse because as a minister, they depend on you. Whether you're a pastor or preacher, you have to pass on this anointing from God to others by the Holy Spirit, but if you do not have that encouragement, you will not be able to successfully pass it on. It is impossible to give what you do not have.

While Peter and John were going to the synagogue to pray, they encountered an ungodly man who was lame and poor. Fixing his eyes on him, Peter said to him: "Silver and gold I do not have, but what I do have I give you" (Acts 3:6). And this man, lame from birth, was healed, because he could benefit from what Peter and John had. Friend, brother, if we are paralyzed, we will never be able to give what we do not have. I believe the most painful thing is knowing that we are not giving to others what we should be giving them simply because we are paralyzed. The greatest danger of paralysis is that it doesn't allow the body to feel pain. Pain serves as a warning from the body, which lets you know something is wrong. Pain also serves to let you know there's danger or something is abnormal. When the nerves are damaged, the body is at risk. The lack of feeling can cause serious problems. I have heard of people who suffered severe burns on their bodies just because they couldn't feel heat. One of the serious effects of spiritual paralysis is that at times it hinders us from hearing (sensing) the voice of the Holy Spirit. We can be in the presence of God and not feel Him. Nor can we feel His conviction or His consuming love. David cried out to God when he stopped feeling the joy of his salvation because he was paralyzed by his sin. It is necessary that we know God's attributes. The Word says that Jehovah will not despise a contrite and humble heart. When paralysis takes control of the soul, it is impossible to feel sad. When we pray, we feel far from God; we feel that our prayer isn't even going up, as if above us are brass heavens and walls of iron that don't allow God to enter or our prayers to escape. We constantly battle with the fact that we don't have any feeling. Many say: "It's just that I don't feel anything." I agree that our relationship with God is not based on our feelings; it is a walk of faith. We know that times of testing will come, and we have to persevere until we receive an answer. That is something that is very common in the normal life of a believer, but when all feeling is lost for months or years because of a trauma, we have to understand that this is not God's normal plan. Examine yourself right now. Are you battling with indifference? Do you know that you have to forgive, but you don't *feel* like doing it? Should you love, but you don't *feel* like doing it? Should you trust, but you don't *feel* like doing it? Should you ask for forgiveness, but you don't *feel* like doing it?

The Word of God teaches us how we should live, think, and act. Having difficulty in obeying the biblical commandments should be sufficient reason to concern us. Paralysis is frustrating. It is used by the enemy of our souls to make you feel useless regarding the calling, service, and purpose God has predestined for you.

The swelling. As if the pain and the paralysis weren't enough, the third stage is the swelling. The dictionary defines the word *swelling* as an "enlargement caused by internal pressure." When Paul was attacked by the viper, everyone was waiting for him to swell up. The physical evidence that the victim was going to die was the swelling. Swelling is caused by the accumulation of water and toxins that the body retains when the natural filters no longer function. Kidneys are the body's filter. They purify the blood and cleanse the water. The blood depends on these organs to maintain its function and provide life. The type of venom from these vipers causes swelling because the kidneys stop functioning, so the body becomes poisoned, which ends up causing death.

The enemy knows that if we give him a legal right to open a door, he will assume total control in order to poison us next. Ephesians 5:26 teaches us that the Word of God will "cleanse [us] with the washing of water by the word." The enemy will desperately try to put you in a situation where your "kidneys" cannot function. The "kidneys" of the believer is the Word of God. The Word is the filter for our spirit, soul, and body. Is it a coincidence that the first thing that we stop doing when we're attacked is the reading of the Word of God? We can read newspapers, magazines, books, and even spend entire hours in front of the television. But when it's time to read the Bible, we are suddenly overcome with irresistible tiredness and discouragement. We not only stop reading the Bible, but we also stop believing it, confessing it, and using it. When we stop reading, believing, and confessing the Word of God, it becomes impossible to apply it to our lives. The devil knows what Psalm 1 says: "And in His law (the Word of God) he meditates day and night. He shall be like a tree planted by the rivers of water, that brings forth its fruit in its season, whose leaf also shall not wither" (vv. 2–3). Satan is the one who causes spiritual droughts in your life. He dries up hearts, marriages, and ministries. The benefits of knowing the Word of God are plentiful. When you guard the Word of God in your heart, and obey it, then what Joshua 1:8 says will happen: "For then you will make your way prosperous, and then you will have good success." With this truth in mind, it is essential that our spiritual "kidneys" continue to function normally.

The venom causes the kidneys to stop functioning, and the Word of God stops having an effect in your life. Before the attack came to traumatize you, the Word of God was the anchor of your soul. But when the venom spread throughout your body, you stopped reading, believing, meditating, and applying the Word of God to your daily life. For many believers, the Bible is an historic and theological book that usually accompanies them to church and nothing more. Nevertheless, when you study the birth and development of the early church, you will notice that during that historical time period a countless number of believers dedicated their lives to copying the original biblical manuscripts, allowing them to be passed from one generation to the next. These men sacrificed their lives and spilt their blood to preserve the Word of God.

The danger is in not reading and believing the Word of God. Why? Because this Word is the foundation of our faith (Romans 10:17). It is the anchor of our promises. Our prayers, intercessions, pleas, and supplications are backed up by this sacred manual of instructions called the Word of God. Within its pages is found our inheritance and instructions to live and obey our Lord.

His complete plan and will for our lives are in the Bible. Without discounting the dreams and supernatural visions, the Holy Scriptures are the primary way that God communicates with His people.

I am convinced that many Christians today die spiritually because they do not have a strong biblical foundation. In the same way, many believers have not obtained God's promises because they have stopped applying the Word to their lives. Jesus said: "If you abide in Me, and My words abide in you, you will ask what you desire, and it shall be done for you" (John 15:7).

The common denominator to receive what we ask for is conditional: "If His Word remains in us, let us ask whatever we want," not what we need. How will God give everything that I want? The secret is when we abide in Him and His Word abides in us, we are going to ask Him in accordance with His perfect will. We know His will because He is in us. The will of God is in His Word. If we read and apply it, we will not have to worry about asking for something outside of His will or asking for something against His will.

Once the Word of God is no longer being read because of

the venom, our lives begin to swell up. They swell up because the internal pressures have disfigured and contaminated us.

At times, the attacks and traumas disfigure us, and we no longer look like the person God created. Once we swell up and portray the disfiguration that comes with this condition, we stop representing the image and likeness of God Almighty. Just as our body fills up with toxins, our emotional life also becomes contaminated with other types of toxins: doubt, fear, anxiety, hate, rancor, resentment, low self-esteem, depression, and others. *The Oxford Dictionary* tells us that toxins are caused by the venom. If these toxins remain in your system without the Word of God functioning as a purifier and filter, your spiritual life will end because of failing, and every dream you have in your spiritual bosom will be aborted.

The Word of God is also our mirror (James 1:23–24). Besides studying it, I like to use it to examine and see my reflection like a mirror. If what is reflected in the mirror is not what God designed for me, I know I'm in grave danger and need divine instruction and His immediate help.

At this point I would like you to pause and take a look at your life. What is your reflection like?

Are you pleased with what you see in the mirror, or do you notice that it isn't what the Lord planned for you? My prayer is that the Holy Spirit shows you the will of the Father and the divine plan that He ordained for you.

Asphyxiation. The last phase of the attack is asphyxiation. Generally speaking, that is the cause of death. The asphyxiation is caused by the suffocation. Suffocation occurs when you're not inhaling sufficient oxygen. This happens when the venom causes swelling, which hinders the oxygen from flowing through the respiratory tract. The trachea is the track that oxygen uses to enter through the mouth or the nose to the lungs. With swelling, this track closes up due to the pressure, and the person lapses into a state of unconsciousness before dying. Fighting for breath is a desperate and agonizing moment. Something that was so natural to do, such as breathing, now turns into a fight for life or death.

The track we use to breathe and keep ourselves alive is our relationship with God. Our relationship with God is what keeps us alive and joyful in Christ. The anchor of our soul is being able to wake up each morning with life to pray and praise our God. When someone enters this last stage of not being able to communicate or breathe as before, it is cause for desperation and becoming anxious and fearful. We do not realize until now how natural it was to inhale and exhale. Medical science describes these actions of inhaling and exhaling as involuntary movements. This means that, without thinking about it beforehand, we inhale and exhale involuntarily; they are automatic actions or reflexes. In the same manner, when we are living according to His perfect will, it is absolutely natural to breathe the breath of God.

The stage of asphyxiation is divided into three phases: the fight to breathe, unconsciousness, and death.

The fight to breathe. The fight with the respiratory tract happens because of a tracheal blockage. What is blocking your life that hinders you from having communion with God? What is hindering the closeness you had before and that you now long to return to? Now you find yourself in the stage where you feel that with each second that goes by you're losing strength, courage, and hope. You see others around you laughing and breathing with great ease. You ask yourself: "What's wrong with me?" Then you find yourself in a stage even more desperate. You're unconscious.

Unconsciousness. When you enter the stage of unconsciousness, you stop fighting. Your strength and courage have left you. You feel totally helpless. You are focusing on the words the devil has whispered in your ears that say: "You have lost everything: your spiritual inheritance, your marriage, your youth, your integrity, your ministry, your dreams, and your destiny." And even though you're not interested in listening to the opinion of the enemy, you have no other choice because you are spiritually and emotionally unconscious.

Death. Finally, death comes—separation—which is the last stage. Not able to receive oxygen, your heart stops beating. Death is the stage when the spirit separates from the physical body. When you die spiritually, the devil is the one who assumes final control. You are separated. When you die spiritually, you are at the mercy of your body, which means that all the decisions and plans for your earthly life are directed by the carnal man. It is sad to see someone make impulsive and rash decisions. I have known a good number of believers who were obedient and on fire about God's plan, but then allowed the enemy to disconnect them from the "respiratory tract," which is the presence of Jehovah. Death is one of the saddest things. Knowing that the person has been taken to another place, where they will be separated eternally, is reason for sadness. Even though, from a human perspective, we know that a brother or sister in the faith or a family member has a better destiny after death, it still brings tears and pain, but what will happen to that person who does not have the hope of a better destiny?

The Spirit of God, who dwells in us, cries and sympathizes with his people when they allow the enemy to determine their spiritual death. Jesus said that Satan came to steal, kill, and destroy (John 10:10). This spiritual death separates you totally from God. The sad thing about it is that at times we believe that because we belong to a church or its council, we are exempt from spiritual death. There are preachers who are preaching from catacombs because they are nothing more than spiritual cadavers. They do not have a fresh word or an anointing that follows them because their relationship with God is dead. The reason we don't feel anything in services where God's presence is present is because we're dead, and the dead cannot feel. Emotional death is equally dangerous. Your emotions consist of your mind, will, and desires. When you die emotionally, it is impossible to fulfill God's plan for your life.

There are women who suffer from an inferiority complex because of their husbands, and they have not been able to recover their emotional health. Spiritually they are fine, they are active in the church, and they persevere, but their emotions have not been healed. Daily they remember and relive traumas that cause them pain in their private life. The devil lies to them, saying they have to act like clowns, smiling on the outside, but crying on the inside. Some become experts in hiding their pain so that they can perform their tasks and responsibilities.

Emotional death is sad because we cannot apply the Word of God to our lives and be in a place where we can receive the blessings God wants to give to us. An example of this is what the Bible refers to in Ephesians 1:3: "Blessed be the God and Father of our Lord Jesus Christ, who has blessed us with every spiritual blessing in the heavenly places in Christ." It is impossible to receive and apply this continual blessing if we do not allow it to be conveyed to our mind. Ephesians 4:23 says: ". . . and be renewed in the spirit of your mind." Since we are more than conquerors through the One who loved us, we have to allow our spirit access to our emotions no matter what kinds of situations threaten us. God has given us His powerful Word so that it is available to us, but we have to meditate on it day and night (Joshua 1:8) so that everything goes well for us as we truly prosper. Our mind plays an important role in obtaining and maintaining the victory. We must bring to pass the victories that belong to us according to the Word of God. Dr. Tim Warner says:

1. Your mind tells you: "You are a sinner because you sin."

The Word says: "You are a saint (whom God has declared righteous) who sins."

2. Your mind tells you: "You are what you do." The Word says: "You were made in the image and likeness of God."

3. Your mind tells you: "Your identity comes from what people say about you." The Word says: "Your identity comes from what the Lord says about you."

4. You mind tells you: "Your conduct tells you what you should believe about yourself." The Word says: "Your belief about yourself determines your conduct."

"For as he thinks in his heart, so is he" (Proverbs 23:7). The key word is *think*. If you let your thoughts run with the wind, you will never have thoughts shaped and molded by God's Word. It is crucial that our identity be healthy and anchored in the Word of God. The believer who has his thoughts filtered by the Word of God possesses a healthy and correct perspective and perception before God.

Discussion Questions Chapter 5

1. How can you relate to the pain explained in chapter 5?

2. Can you explain in detail the areas of your life that are paralyzed?

3. How did the "swelling" manifest itself during the attack?

4. How do you deal with the "asphyxiations" in your life?

5. Write down four things you could do to counter the following phases:

Terminal: _____

_____

_____

Pain: _____

_____

_____

Paralysis: _____

_____

_____

Swelling: _____

_____

_____

Asphyxiation: _____

_____

_____

How can you experience the "zoé" life?

MARK VEGA
JAN. 9, 1970 –

Chapter 6

They're Planning Your Funeral

However, they were expecting that he would swell up or suddenly fall down dead. (Acts 28:6)

God created us for a great purpose. The destroyer of our souls intends to fight tirelessly to destroy the destiny designed by God for your life. However, this destiny ordained by God is conditional. God told Moses: "You shall enter the Promised Land." But because he did not obey God, it was Joshua who entered. God also promised David: "You will build me a temple," but because he also did not obey God, it was his son Solomon who built it. Paul said to Timothy, "This charge I commit to you, son Timothy, according to the prophecies previously made concerning you, that by them you may wage the good warfare" (1 Timothy 1:18). We have to fight so that God's promises are fulfilled in our lives as He wishes.

God assures Moses that He will be with him and will use him to free the people of Israel from the Egyptians. He explains to him what signs and wonders He will perform to confirm His Word so that Pharaoh sees that Moses has Jehovah's backing. But suddenly, God gets mad with Moses and looks for him to kill him. What happens between verses 23 and 24 in the fourth chapter of Exodus? God delights in Moses, and first He commissions him to carry orders to confront Pharaoh; then, he looks for Moses to kill him. His wife Zipporah takes a sharp flint stone and circumcises his son and throws the baby's foreskin at Moses' feet. This intervention by Zipporah appeases God, who then has mercy on Moses.

Moses seemed to think that because he had an intimate relationship with Jehovah, he did not have to circumcise his son on the eighth day according to the Jewish laws. Nevertheless he was under a wrong impression just as many ministers are today. They believe that their many years in the ministry exempt them from obeying God's law. At times we believe that the more titles we gain or the more years we have in the ministry, the more freedom we have to take shortcuts or detours. We err when we do not obey the laws or commandments given by God. Notice well that although God had called Moses and promised to use him to free His people, now he seeks him to kill him. Don't take lightly God's call or His promises made to you; let us be obedient to please God in everything. You control your own destiny.

When Paul is attacked by the viper, everyone expected him to fall over dead. The enemy of our souls waits for you to fail. He wants to get rid of you as soon as possible. Considering all that has happened in your life, the devil is planning your funeral. Seeing all those who have gone before us who have fallen and died, I can imagine and see the people who surrounded Paul in that instant, saying to one another: "Go look for the shovels. Prepare a place for his burial." All of them were expecting him to die. It's possible that even some of them wanted him to suffer a slow death, because they believed it was God's judgment on him. Others, perhaps, were rejoicing for what awaited him. And even others didn't care about the manner in which he would die. During the chaos that suddenly happened because of the incident, a crowd began to form to see what would happen next. All of them were waiting for Paul to die. It is probable that they began to measure the time it would take to bury this man called Paul. They waited and waited and continued to wait.

It is incredible how this event can seem to resemble the attacks in our own lives. The devil, with all his army, and without knowing the future, puts a lot of attention on how you react when you are attacked so he can celebrate later. If you want to hurt the devil, worship God in the midst of the storm. March around your house and glorify God in the midst of the pain. Instead of taking an antidepressant when you feel those symptoms that want to control your mind and your body, look for the Bible and begin to sing psalms to the Lord. Do not give Satan the satisfaction of reacting with fear and insecurity. While you're reading this book, perhaps you're thinking about the current attack you are going through. I want you to know that during these difficult and incomprehensible times, God is on your side and with the faithfulness of a true friend, He wants to help you.

While you're going through trial by fire, the demons are celebrating. While you're reading this book, your enemies are preparing your funeral. They are rehearsing the eulogy they will recite in front of your grave. Others will shine your coffin, smiling and screaming their heads off: "Finally, _____ (your name) has died! He'll no longer cause us migranes . We'll no longer have to reinforce our gates because of him."

Our enemies are not just spiritual; they are are also carnal enemies (Psalm 3). They are buying their black suit so they can parade at your funeral. They are preparing your headstone; they're practicing their condolences.

Look around you carefully. All of them are present at your funeral. The devil and his demons, your enemies, are all celebrating. The headstone has your name and your birth date inscribed along with the predicted date of your spiritual death. The enemy put it there. They have dug the hole, and those who have witnessed the last scene of your life are anxious for the funeral home director to begin the funeral service. Everyone is ready. Preparations have been made, and the enemy is happy; however, there's a problem . . .

The coffin is empty. Are you ready to die? Ask yourself this question, because you are the one who controls your destiny. God has provided you with everything necessary for you to live according to John 10:10. There is nothing worse than feeling the pain of rejection. When you see everyone celebrating your death, you feel the cruelty of such an act. Christ can sympathize and identify with your pain. During the last twelve hours, from the moment He was arrested in the garden of Gethsemane, Jesus suffered mocking and was beaten. The Jewish people, whom He came to seek and save, were the first to condemn him to death. If there is anyone who can sympathize with our weaknesses, it's Christ, the Savior of the world. His Word says that He was tempted in everything. I'm sure that Jesus was tempted to not want to die when he prayed to the Father, saying: "O My Father, if it is possible, let this cup pass from Me; nevertheless not as I will but as You will" (Matthew 26:39). Jesus is asking the Father to free him from the torment. The most precious gift God gives to human beings is free will. Self-will, the freedom to choose for ourselves. It is a powerful weapon that God has given to humanity. The heart of God fills with happiness when by our own will we surrender to Him so that He does with us whatever He wills.

"He gave His only begotten Son, that whoever believes in Him should not perish but have everlasting life" (John 3:16). Now it is our turn to accept or reject. We have the power to make the decision to continue as good soldiers of the faith or give up on the journey. Jesus said: "The kingdom of heaven suffers violence, and the violent take it by force" (Matthew 11:12). Notice those who have determined not to lose but to win; those who are going to receive their reward from God. I want to tell you that your victory lies in your determination not to lose. The woman who suffered from a flow of blood opted not to die. By her persistent faith she obtained her healing, and although she practically had to crawl, she made a way through the crowd that surrounded her. Without doubt, in her intent to reach Jesus, she was criticized, kicked, had dirt thrown in her face, and suffered humiliation. Nevertheless, she held on to her decision firmly. And through her fervor and pushing, she succeeded in receiving her miracle. She was rewarded with virtue and healing from the Lord. Blind Bartimaeus received his sight, but he had to cry out until the Lord heard him.

Christ voluntarily stripped Himself of His glory, His omnipresence, His omniscience, His omnipotence. Like a lamb He was carried to the slaughterhouse. When Peter cut off Malchus' right ear, the servant to the high priest, Jesus rebuked him, saying: "Do you think I cannot now pray to My

Father, and he will provide Me with more than twelve legions of angels?" (Matthew 26:53).

In this incidence, Jesus reveals the essence of His voluntary humility and how He keeps Himself in the perfect will of the Father.

In His omniscience, the Father has seen your pain. He knows the horrific events you have suffered, but in spite of all of that, the enemy still cannot invade or manipulate your will. You must make the decision for yourself to continue until you reach the next level with God. Friend, take a look at what has happened to you. Consider the course of your life; it has been painful, but with purposes ordained by God. You cannot give up now. If you believe, you will see God's purpose manifest itself in its right time.

Hang in there! If you keep on fighting to resist the evil one, I assure you that in the right time God will take responsibility for honoring you.

Several years ago I spoke to a cardiologist, and he explained to me that a young person has less chance of surviving a heart attack than an older person. That's because as a person grows older, their heart builds new veins. Those veins are called subsidiary veins. The expression *subsidiary guarantee* is very popular among the financial institutions that measure the value of possessions that their clients have accumulated over time. While the heart beats millions of times over a long period, it builds new veins that are absolutely necessary. If an adult suffers a heart attack, the subsidiary veins absorb the most impact, saving the person from greater damage. Even though the heart of a young person is much stronger than an older person, when they suffer a heart attack, it is fatal in the majority of cases because they lack those subsidiary veins. "And we know that all things work together for good" (Romans 8:28). With each circumstance that comes to your life, be it an attack, a trauma, a fight or a test, remember that whatever it is, you are building subsidiary veins. Without realizing it, you're developing a stronger anointing that will counter the attacks of the enemy in the name of Jesus Christ. Don't look at your enemies, because you will surely become discouraged. I am convinced that Paul said to himself: "You called me to suffer for your Name, to preach Your Word to the Gentiles, and to the kings and sons of Israel; Your mission for my life still has not ended."

Paul understands he has a special calling on his life, and the devil is in no way happy about it. In that crucial moment, Paul does not waste his time in looking at those who were present: he looks to the future, the plan, purpose, and mission God has for his life. Considering the entirety of God's plan and the role he was to play in that plan, Paul was not ready to die.

Examine your life now and think about what God has freed you from. Do you believe your life should end this way? There is a purpose and a plan that still have not totally come to pass. The present attack, just like the one that helped Paul fulfill his ministry, will help to shape you to be the kind of person God can use. Don't let this present attack destroy you. Use it as an experience and determine in your spirit to persevere until the end. Refuse to live, pray, and act according to what others say or try to pressure you to do. I prefer to live according to what God says and thinks about me and not what the present situation is dictating, for it will soon pass away.

The Decision Is Yours

Paul makes the decision to live and not to die—and also to believe God. What decision will you choose? Even though you have experienced a shipwreck, storm, cold, rain, and a snake bite, God has stayed by your side, ready to free you from every unexplainable thing. Many of us do not understand what is happening to us, but God sees it and understands everything. He is waiting for you to decide what you're going to do: either continue in His plan or abandon everything. God cannot operate nor manifest Himself in your life unless you decide not to die. Invite Him to show His power in your life. He promises not to despise a contrite and humble heart.

Chapter 6 Questions

1. What are some major attacks you are suffering right now?
2. Explain the term *subsidiary veins*. In what ways are they beneficial?
3. Are you ready to die before seeing your miracle?
4. Describe three ways in which you have decided to live.
5. In what way will you invite God to demonstrate His power in your life?
6. What do you see about God's plan, purpose, and mission for your life when you look at the future?

Chapter 7

The Antidote

That good thing which was committed to you, keep by the Holy Spirit who dwells in us. (2 Timothy 1:14)

What did Paul possess that did not allow him to die like any other victim? I often ask myself: What did the early church possess that enabled them to refuse the temptation to deny their faith? They had resolve of spirit that made them willing to face any persecution even unto death. The history of martyrs tells of entire families that were devoured by lions just for refusing to deny their faith. The history of the Christian martyrs that suffered torture is still a well-known subject among many people—accounts of men and women who were willing to use their final moments for an eternal purpose. Jesus did the same in His final moments. I can picture the disciples, with tears in their eyes, as they listened attentively to His last words. Luke writes in his Gospel (24:49) what Jesus said to His disciples: "Behold, I send the Promise of My Father upon you; but tarry in the city of Jerusalem until you are endued with power from on high." Perhaps they asked: "Power? What power, and why?" Luke also tells us in Acts 1:8 what the last words of Jesus on earth were: "But you shall receive power when the Holy Spirit has come upon you; and you shall be witnesses to Me in Jerusalem, and in all Judea and Samaria, and to the end of the earth." It is interesting that the word *witnesses* is *martus* in Greek, which is translated *martyr*.

After studying that, I understood that Jesus knew they would give their lives for Him, and, in the natural, they would not go forward a single step without being filled with divine power. The power on the Day of Pentecost came to the Upper Room when they were all baptized with the Holy Spirit; finally, those believers gave their lives for the cause of the gospel. When we compare the times from the past with the present, we see there has been a falling away from the responsibility of evangelization, not only in the church but also among believers. Many people today have neighbors they have never spoken with about the gospel. We work or study with unbelievers, and we don't dare to speak to them about Christ. We are surrounded by people for whom awaits an eternity of doom in hell and we ignore the subject completely, because of shame or it being a bother. Just thinking about moving out of our comfort zone causes us discomfort. I would say that we as pastors are the cause for this dilemma. We have defined the Holy Spirit as an object or a thing, but not as a person. Metaphorically, the Bible uses symbols (wind, dove, fire, water, oil, rivers of living water) in order to give a description of His attributes, but we have not taught about His personality. The Holy Spirit is the third Person of the Trinity, and He is God. God is not only *with* us or *for* us, but God is *in* us. Think about it in this way: God living in you! Paul did not fall victim to the serpent because God was with him. When the bush was burning in the desert next to Mount Sinai, the miracle was not the fact that a voice was heard coming out of it, but rather that the bush was not consumed by the fire. The major thing is not that you're going through a fire. The miraculous thing about it is that in the midst of the fire you continue to reflect the image of God. First Corinthians 10:13

says: "No temptation has overtaken you except such as is common to man." Tribulations in the life of a believer should be expected. What we need to be sure of is that we are covered by the shade that is much higher than the tribulation. The reason why the bush was not consumed was because God was in it. God did not free Shadrach, Meshach, and Abednego *from* the fire; instead, He protected them and freed them *in* the fire. ". . . *it is* for your consolation and salvation" (2 Corinthians 1:6). The Holy Spirit has been given to this world to bring conviction of sin, to call sinners to have an encounter with Christ, and also to empower the church to live intentionally, to be soul winners, and to witness without fear. The Holy Spirit was more than religion in the life of Paul; He was a Person who shared an intimate relationship with the Apostle. Without divine empowering, Paul would not have been able to survive that fierce attack.

Without Paul two-thirds of the New Testament would not have been written, the church never would have been formed, and neither would God's plan have become a reality. Paul did not understand his future. He did not know what God's exact plan for his life was, but he for sure knew there was a plan for him.

Perhaps you do not understand why the devil has attacked you so intensely; why you have had to fight since your childhood to survive, and why death has tried so hard to take you. Why have traumas, bad experiences, and mental attacks, family, social and financial troubles suddenly come upon you? It's not because God hates you; on the contrary, it's because God will use every negative experience to glorify Himself in you. God uses the worst of our life so we can empathize with others who are going through the same things we have gone through. That is why the Bible says that we are an open letter, because we have been created so the world can read us and know that by the grace of God we have survived. We go through fire, death, tragedies, traumas, but we still are on our feet, trusting in the God who keeps His promises. Years later, Paul wrote to the church in Rome: "For I consider that the sufferings of this present time are not worthy to be compared with the glory which shall be revealed in us" (Romans 8:18).

God wants to use us to win others through our tears, battles, and pains. Our pain and our trials are the most powerful factors to win others for Christ because they counteract the message the enemy pitches to the world, which says, "No one understands. You're all alone in your pain."

God has delivered us from a specific area so that we can free others who are in the same condition. It's important to notice that the area where you were previously wounded now has greater power and anointing than the other areas of your life. No one can relate, sympathize, or minister to a young girl who is contemplating having an abortion better than the person who has gone through a similar situation; someone who has seen the hand of God bring forgiveness, healing, and restoration to their life. A diamond, in its original state, is coal. Coal is ugly; it has nothing attractive about it and is dirty. No one puts on a ring or jewelry made of coal. Never has a woman been seen using a chain with coal hanging from her neck. As previously mentioned in this book, in order to change into a diamond, the coal has to go through a process: it has to endure excessive pressure and heat, and not for a day or for a year, but rather for decades. The process is extensive and detailed. As it goes through the process, the coal has to maintain its integrity and not break up. If it comes apart during the process, it will never reach its potential of becoming a diamond. It has to endure the process and maintain its integrity and not allow the heat and pressure to rob it from being the most precious stone of the planet.

If Paul had fallen apart during the moment of attack, he never would have become the treasure God would use to revolutionize the world. Years later, he would write in one of his letters: "But we have this treasure in earthen vessels . . ." (2 Corinthians 4:7). There is no doubt that he understood that his life was a process of formation: from coal to diamond. You should ask yourself: How is my spiritual formation coming along? Am I sparkling through the process, or am I wasting the opportunity God has given me to reach my destiny and His plan for my life? God knows that alone we could never carry out His plan. That's why He has given the antidote so we don't die or fall apart during the difficult times. Remember, God will not allow us to be tempted more than we can resist; but with the temptation He will give us the way of escape. Don't be tempted to give up and throw in the towel. Resist the temptation and take the antidote. Fight, battle, and resist the desires that could disqualify you from later being used with greater strength. If you're going through a situation or deadly attack right now, remember that although you can't see the venom, this attack is for your consolation and salvation. You will soon be rejoicing and celebrating this problem that has brought tears to your life. Your sorrow will turn into a rejoicing , your sadness into joy, but all this depends on you staying in the process without fail. Don't fall apart!

The Presence of the Holy Spirit Living in You

The fact that God lives in us makes us the "majority" over our economic level, race, culture, or physical appearance. As stated before, I've never seen someone assaulting a vagabond; only people who are carrying something of value with them. The fact that God lives in you makes you a candidate to be attacked by the enemy. He doesn't want you to reach for the stars, future directions, goals, and desires God has placed in your heart. When the Holy Spirit lives in you, you have the advantage of being victorious every time the enemy tries to attack you to cause you damage or losses. When the Holy Spirit lives inside you, He keeps you so you don't become contaminated with the sin of this world. A fish can live for years in salt water, but when you take it out of the water and prepare it in the kitchen, you have to add salt to it so it has flavor. How can that be? During all those years it lived and swam in salt water, it never became contaminated. It did not become contaminated because its scales, which are its natural defenses, protected its body. The fish's defenses protected it from being contaminated. So it is with the Spirit who lives in you. He keeps you from sin and spiritual death. When the Holy Spirit lives inside you, He makes you aware of His presence.

I believe that the times we have fallen into sin, it has not been intentional, but rather because we have forgotten to access His presence that lives in us. When we become desensitized to sin or play with temptations, the "serpents" abound and we play with fire. That's when the presence of the Holy Spirit is quenched in our consciences. This causes the powerful presence of God to live hidden in our subconscious and subsequently causes some door in our lives to be wide open and thus at the mercy of attacks and sin.

The church of today has forgotten that the presence of the Holy Spirit indwells us. This is evident in what we see on television, by the music we listen to, in the lies that come out of our mouths, and in what we allow our eyes to see. The lack of integrity among God's people today is an additional sign that we have not fallen under the conviction of the Holy Spirit, who professedly lives in us.

Some years ago a bracelet that read "What would Jesus Do?" (WWJD) came out on the market. It helped to remind young people of the indwelling presence of Jesus in them; to motivate them to imagine the following: If Jesus were here in this world, what would He do in certain circumstances? The question would help people make decisions according to what Jesus would do. It also helped us to remember what Jesus would do if he were in our shoes. What decision would He make? I don't see anything wrong with this; I simply believe we should recognize that our convictions to live rightly before God without being tainted by sin should originate not just with a bracelet, but in our relationship with the Holy Spirit, who lives in us. The Holy Spirit is not a magic amulet, but Someone who lives in each of us in order to give testimony of Jesus Christ; to help us in our weaknesses and empower us to be more than conquerors.

Paul knew that the presence of God lived inside him, and so he felt confident and secure; he recognized that God held the plan for his life in His hands. There was no reason to fear or feel insecure. When we discover that the Almighty and All Powerful God lives in us, that is when we will understand that we were created to be conquerors and overcomers. Failure and defeat are not in God's plan for us. God has programmed us to be overcomers. Jude 24 says: "Now to Him who is able to keep you from stumbling, and to present you faultless before the presence of His glory with exceeding joy."

David said that we are arrows in the hands of the archer. God is aiming us toward the camp of the enemy. The arrows were prepared by a process using a hammer, fire, and sharpening. Your life has been hammered, sharpened, and set on fire, melted and then molded by very unpleasant circumstances, but smile and trust God to uphold you in His hand. He is the Archer. The Archer will not miss. We have been made to tear down the enemy's forces. Trust in God in spite of what is happening in your life right now. Rest now, because your Archer knows you have been perfected for the mission.

What determines that the arrow will reach its target is its resistance against the bowstring. There has to be resistance to give strength to shoot the arrow. Do you realize now why the resistance in your life has been necessary? God is preparing to use you to destroy your enemies. Take courage. God has you in His hands, and you will soon see the greatest victory in your life. Resistance is what is going to speed up your journey to victory. It's possible in this very moment that God is tightening the bowstring in order to fashion in us good character, discipline, integrity, and power. He knows when to "shoot" us, but He wants to be sure that in the middle of the journey you do not lose the strength to reach your target. If you lose thrust, you will not reach the goal or the assigned target. It's necessary for God to "pull" us until He is sure we have what is needed to faithfully complete the mission.

Security and Confidence in God
Is His Plan for My Life

"Those who trust in the LORD are like Mount Zion, which cannot be moved, but abides forever. As the mountains surround Jerusalem, so the LORD surrounds His people from this time forth and forever" (Psalm 125:1–2). You are, in singular or plural form, Mount Zion. We are the church of Jesus Christ. Zion was built upon a rock. Its foundation is firm and permanent. We, the church of Christ, have also been built on the Rock. Mount Zion is so valuable that our security is impenetrable, and the gates of hell will not prevail against it. Those who trust in Jehovah are firmly established on the promises of God. Psalm 125:1 says, "[They] are like Mount Zion."

They cannot be removed by the prince of the air, nor by his army or his strategies. They will not be shaken from their integrity or their confidence in God. When we learn to trust in God, He will put mountains around us; giving us the security to think differently. God is our "refuge and strength, a very present help in trouble" (Psalm 46:1). He promises to take care of us. "If He takes care of the birds, He will also take care of you," the poet assures us. And Isaiah 44:2 says that before we were even conceived, God had a plan prepared for us. He will help us fulfill His purposes according to His perfect will. When I think about this important truth, I receive encouragement and courage because I understand that everything I have suffered in my past was, in the end, to prepare me for today. I don't have to ask God why. If I was born poor in a dysfunctional family, suffering abuses, I reflect on the fact that God is with me and surrounds me with His divine protection. This is important in our development, because when someone offends us, mistreats us, or betrays us, it's not to stop us from serving God or to lead us astray, but rather for our consolation and our salvation (2 Corinthians 1:6). Each past or future incident is permitted by God to let us know that God loves us and wants to free us.

Don't Expect Me to Die!

But after they had looked for a long time and saw no harm come to him, they changed their minds. (Acts 28:6)

In this very moment, the enemy is watching you. He wants to know if you are going to give up or if you are going to continue on this difficult road. "The devil walks about like a roaring lion, seeking whom he may devour" (1 Peter 5:8). *Seeking* is an interesting word. The Bible teaches us that God looks for worshipers who will worship Him in spirit and truth. "For the eyes of the LORD run to and fro throughout the whole earth, [seeking] to show Himself strong on behalf of those whose heart is loyal to Him" (2 Chronicles 16:9, added by author).

As long as we don't recognize this point, we're not going to react correctly. We have an audience watching us. They want to see how we are going to react. Hebrews 12:1 says: "Therefore we also, since we are surrounded by so great a cloud of witnesses, let us lay aside every weight, and the sin which so easily ensnares us, and let us run with endurance the race that is set before us." Surrounded by so great a cloud of witnesses, heaven is watching us, and the angels too. Just as we have a great cloud of witnesses, we also have a great cloud of enemies, murderers, who in the same way are observing us to condemn us.

We are told in Acts 19:15 that the sons of Sceva, wandering exorcists, tried to free a demoniac. But when they confronted the demon, he told them: "Jesus I know, and Paul I know; but who are you?" I tell you the following with my strongest conviction: Satan is not omnipresent, nor omniscient, nor omnipotent; but he is very astute and shrewd. Paul tells us not to be ignorant concerning the devil's ambushes and traps. The satanic kingdom is strategic and wants you to walk in your flesh. The carnal life interprets every event and trauma the wrong way. The carnal mind observes every trauma, attack, injustice, abuse, and decides: "No more! It's not worth it. It's not worth the sacrifice or the waste of time."

Doctors say that when a person is about to die, they are released from the earthly to enter the eternal. In the same way, with this book in your hands, you have the power to die now or continue fighting and conquering ground for the Lord. Those who were surrounding Paul on that island waited a long time for the apostle to die. In the same way, the devil waits for you to die as well. I can picture the demons, hand in hand, looking to see if Paul's future would be snuffed out, if the promise concerning him would cease, if the Timothys in the faith would go without a mentor and spiritual father. The enemy not only takes notice of the present, but he also takes notice of the Lord's future and complete plan for your present and future life. There are people you are going to impact. A generation is waiting for the rod of authority. Don't let it fall down.

Discussion Questions for Chapter 7

1. How can you relate to the "antidote"?
2. What role does the Holy Spirit play in your personal life?
3. What areas qualify as "fire," and which ones as "pressure" in the process coal goes through to become a diamond?
4. Describe three ways that make you feel that you are in the process of being transformed from a piece of coal into a diamond.
5. What practical principles can you apply from Jude 24?
6. What message will you send to your enemies who are waiting for your death?

7. Just as Paul did with Timothy when he left him his spiritual legacy, can you name a "Timothy" God has put in your life so that in the same way you can transfer to that person the same legacy?

MARK VEGA
JAN. 9, 1970 –

Chapter 8

Only a Scar Remains

. . . for I bear in my body the marks of the Lord Jesus.
(Galatians 6:17)

When Paul begins his ministry as apostle, pastor, evangelist, teacher, and prophet, he carries with him a reminder of how God had spared him from death: a scar on his hand. With every letter he writes (two-thirds of the New Testament are made up of his thirteen epistles), he undoubtedly reflects on how God has been with him. While he writes from jail, the flames of the candle light up the scar on his hand. The scar—marked by two tiny holes from the fangs of the viper—is a seminary, a message, and a reminder of the plan and mission of God for his life. The powerful message of the scar is "I suffered it, I survived it, and now I have a license to talk about it."

When he prayed with his hands raised, he saw the marks that the serpent had left on his hand. This gave him inspiration to keep going forward without caring about what he was experiencing at that moment. He knew that the same God who had healed his painful and bleeding wounds was also going to heal his painful and distressful situation. God would continue being glorified in spite of the circumstance.

As he laid his hands on the sick and each time he saw that scar, he no doubt received more inspiration and faith. When he laid his hands on Timothy (2 Timothy 1:6), he not only prayed for an anointing to empower him, but also that he would receive an impartation of tenacity and strength to resist every attack against him. When he laid his hands on believers so they would receive the Holy Spirit, he also asked that the same Spirit heal every wound suffered in the journey of these new converts. When he looked at his hand, the scar transported him back to that unforgettable night (Acts 28:3–6); reminding him of the antidote of the Holy Spirit, who freed him from a sure death. It wasn't possible for any sickness to resist those rivers of faith that flowed from Paul's life. In the times in which we live, scars are considered unpleasant and shameful. Those who have these marks try to get rid of them or hide them. They apply all kinds of makeup creams and even cocoa butter to try to make them disappear. However, the life in Christ is different. The more scars you carry in your body, the more opportunity you will have to honor God for His faithfulness. A scar shows the place where a wound or lesion has been healed. According to *The Oxford Dictionary*, *to heal* is "to unite that which has been cut or broken." Jacob was transformed from a usurper and deceiver to a patriarch. God gave him a new name, a new identity, and a new scar. Along with the inheritance of nations God had given him, Jacob received a wound in his thigh that made him limp for the rest of his life. His scar was not of shame, but of honor and gratefulness to His God. Every step he took was a reminder of his total dependence on God.

This chapter should remain clear in our lives. At times we pray prayers contrary to God's will. We ask Him to make the scars disappear from our lives without understanding that the scar is necessary to bring to pass the destiny God has planned for us. Your prayers will be more fervent, your songs will be more passionate, and your testimony will be more convincing each time you use your scar as a powerful weapon in God.

God wants to heal every lesion in your present life in order to glorify Himself regarding your past. Your present wound will be your future blessing. You will not have to hide the fact that you lost a battle, that you were imperfect, bad, or mistreated; rather, you will show it to the whole world with courage, confidence, and security. The scar on Paul's hand had a history that the entire world needed to hear. Celebrate your scar, because it will be the key that will open doors, cross borders, bring blessings, and resonate with people making it possible for you to relate to those who are going through the same or even worse situations. Learn to talk about and show that scar with authority and confidence.

Remember, the scar is a mark of a healed wound. The antidote of the Holy Spirit and the balm of the Lord Jesus Christ have freed us from what the devil had planned. The evidence we have of this great victory is our scar. Not all scars are the same; rather, all are different. There are no two alike. They come in different sizes and distinct forms. Some are bigger than others. But all have a history to tell. The one who has not discovered the true significance of his scar is wasting a whole life trying to cover it up or hide it. Let us discover our scar and give glory to God for it. Your life will take on an explosive direction when you share your scar and your history with the world. Paul learned to share his scars and understood they were a powerful weapon: ". . . for I bear in my body the marks [scars] of the Lord Jesus" (Galatians 6:17).

Paul never forgot the value of the scars he carried in his body. He always remembered them and made mention of them. He referred to his marks like a good soldier who mentions the medals that have been awarded to him for his excellent military service. He knew that his scars would serve to put into effect the plan and the power of the gospel. However, times have changed and unfortunately scars are not deemed as valuable trophies anymore but as unattractive and embarrassing marks. Our culture would rather hide the scar along with the story in hopes of not having to revisit the memory.

Advertising today tells us that "image is everything;" that is, "Take care of your image and reputation because that is what will open up a way for you in the future." Men don't cry, and women who do are weak and don't understand their rights. Society says: The more fragmented and messed up you are, the fewer opportunities you will have.

Why is it that suffering, pain, or scars are enemies of this progressive generation? In Galatians 3:3, Paul speaks to the church in a tone of exhortation: "Are you so foolish? Having begun in the Spirit, are you now being made perfect by the flesh?" I believe with all my heart that this same urgent rhetoric has to be answered in order to go to the next level. Paul, as a minister of God, doesn't use a credit card as his credentials; rather, he uses his wounds, sufferings, and scars to prove his ministry. The perspective of this servant was that every scar in his body had a history to tell, with the intent that the glory of God be made well-known everywhere.

The process that it takes for a wound to become a scar requires time. Each wound is different. The process is painful, frustrating, and hard at times. But the scar, in the end, is a message to the world that God is faithful, and His mercy is forever. Don't get frustrated when you see that your scar is taking longer than expected to heal. When the skin is torn, the body forms collagenous fibers (proteins) to fill in the lesion and repair the wound, causing the scar. There is no pre-determined time period for the complete healing of that scar. All scars are different. When you suffer an emotional or psychological wound, the balm of prayer, forgiveness, experiences with God, and time itself are the ingredients to repair the wound and heal it.

God always reminded the prophets as well as His people not to forget from where He had delivered them. The reason for this is that a human being is forgetful about what God does for him. We must never forget from where God delivered us, and how close we were to death; how God, at the right time, heard our cry and intervened to help us. When you begin to doubt and forget what God has promised you, look at your scars. Don't see them as something negative, but as a certificate for graduating from the seminary of "pain, bitterness, and anguish," which are your credentials to encourage and help to heal those who are shedding the same tears you used to shed. You will be able to feel compassion for them and be a strong tower so that the world knows that all you have endured and suffered is now just a scar!

Discussion Questions for Chapter 8

1. Describe the most prominent scar of your life.

2. What message does your scar send to the world around you?

3. The powerful message of the scar is: "I _____ it, I_____ it, and now I have a _____ to speak about it."

4. Describe the process of the wound, the healing, and the scar.

5. What did you learn from your scar?

6. What is the greatest danger in trying to cover up a scar?

7. The more _____ you carry in your body, the more _____ you have to honor God for His _____.

Chapter 9

Resurrection Power

In 1948 a man by the name of Ernest Neal was the reason the United States experienced a greater knowledge of the badger. Neal wrote a book titled *The Badger,* which showed the first photo of this little animal.

Part of the reason the badger was discovered so late in history is because by nature it is a nocturnal animal. From Ireland to Japan, the badger increased in number, but its activities were ignored together with its habits.

This mammal is unique in the world. It is known for being loving and caring. Neal frequently says in his book that the badger has been seen adopting litters of skunks when their parents die at the hands of hunters.

There are various classes of badgers I would like to describe to you, but there is one in particular I would like to allude to in this chapter, and that is the "honey badger."

Though docile and humble by nature, the *National Geographic* magazine recognizes it as the fiercest predator that exists. In its 2003 edition, the *Guinness Book of Records* featured the badger as the most daring animal, not only for its aggressiveness or for how dangerous it is, but also for the inner characteristics it possesses. For years, the cobra was considered the most feared creature of the desert, and number two as the most dangerous in the world. When a cobra confronts its victim, it raises its head and prepares to inject its deadly venom. If it's a Mozambique Spitting cobra, it spits in the eyes of its victim to burn the corneas, blinding the victim with venomous toxins before destroying it. Whether it's a lion, gorilla, hyena, or any other animal from the jungle, all of them become victims of the venomous cobra. Although the animal may be dangerous, fierce, or large, it can't resist the deadly venom of the cobra.

As I was describing this venomous snake, I began to notice that its characteristics were similar to those of Satan. The herpetologist C. H. Pope says that "snakes are first cowards, then bluffers, and last of all warriors." They're nocturnal and come in different forms, colors, and sizes. There are thirty-two thousand species of snakes. Some weigh only 8 ounces, while others weigh 320 pounds, reaching a large size of almost 33 feet.

As you can realize, though I'm not a fan of snakes, I have learned several things about them. All the information and facts I got from the *National Geographic* about the cobra never fail to amaze me. The most intriguing, though, was when I learned that the most ferocious animal is not the cobra, but rather the honey badger. How can an animal so docile and loving be catalogued as number one of the most dangerous animals, more so than the scorpion, centipede, or the cobra?

While I was watching television intensely once, I was surprised when I saw what I'm about to tell you. I understood that night that it wasn't a coincidence that I was watching that *National Geographic* program; rather, it was God's purpose to help me finish this book. During the presentation of the new champion of the desert, they showed a battle between a honey badger and the dangerous cobra.

They both move side to side while they stare at each other. They try to strike at each other, but they dodge each other time after time because of the rapid instincts of both predators. The cobra raises its head and begins to move rapidly; suddenly and with intensity he latches on to his opponent and injects him with deadly venom. The badger backs off, losing its strength; nevertheless, the dose of deadly venom that now runs through its body is too much, and he can't resist it.

The cobra begins to move around its victim as it normally does. For a span of three hours, it circles the badger that supposedly is dead. The cobra, nevertheless, does not know that while it's celebrating the supposed death of its victim, something is happening inside the badger's body.

To understand what is happening, you have to know something about the honey badger's nature. During its entire life, it has gotten used to plundering honeycombs in order to feed off its honey. That means it has had to go head to head with bees, and frequently it is attacked and stung by swarms of them. These fights have prepared it for its encounter with the cobra.

While the cobra is celebrating its victory, it doesn't know that the badger, although fallen and unconscious, is making an antidote in its system. The badger, in reality, is not dead. Instead, it is going through a process of transformation. Its body is creating an antidote to counter the deadly dose. Soon it will open its eyes, get up, shake its head violently, and rush to defeat the snake. Now in control of all of its faculties, it will begin to run after the cobra while the snake tries to escape unsuccessfully. The badger catches up to the defenseless and terrorized cobra and with one bite rips off its head and in the end devours it.

"And I will put enmity between you and the woman, and between your seed and her Seed; He shall bruise your head, and you shall bruise His heel" (Genesis 3:15).

Satan took Christ to the cross with the intention of scoffing and shaming him. When Christ died on the cross, Satan had a great celebration over the death of the Son of God. But on the third day, the Spirit of God resurrected Jesus Christ from the dead; He ripped off the head of the devil, and fulfilled the first prophecy of Genesis 3:15. "O Death, where is your sting? O Hades, where is your victory?" (1 Corinthians 15:55).

What prepares the badger for encounters with deadly enemies are the previous attacks and bee stings. Although it doesn't understand the why of the pain from the bee stings and attacks, they are indispensable for its growth, development, and destiny.

I'm sure that at some time you will ask yourself: "Why me? Why that, why my children, why my spouse, why my family, why my finances, why my ministry? Why do the ungodly prosper, and I, a righteous person who fears God, never seem to get ahead?" The psalmist asked himself the same question and concluded that he almost stumbled over it. "But as for me, my feet had almost stumbled; my steps had nearly slipped. For I *was* envious of the boastful, when I saw the prosperity of the wicked" (Psalm 73:2–3).

My prayer for you is that you never forget the honey badger. It could have had lesser probability of winning the battle against the infamous snake, but its past battles with bee stings helped to prepare it for the final victory.

"Now if we are afflicted, *it is* for your consolation and salvation" (2 Corinthians 1:6).

When you cry and shed tears and fight against the tor-
ments of life, don't blame God. I want you to know that it is
during these times of torment there is something happening
inside you that is much more powerful than the external
events. Every attack against your person builds up your spiritual antibodies. Every tear strengthens your faith, and every
time you are scorned by others, it helps to multiply the antidote in your spiritual cells.

"But if the Spirit of Him who raised Jesus from the dead
dwells in you, He who raised Christ from the dead will also
give life to your mortal bodies through His Spirit who dwells
in you" (Romans 8:11).

Paul had the Spirit of God as an antidote living inside him.
In the same way, he constantly suffered pain and bitterness,
which were preparing him to fulfill his destiny and God's purposes. I believe that many of us do not know our final destiny,
but we do understand that we are afflicted, which helps to
shape us to attain what God has prepared for us. Therefore,
let us accept the fights, the tests, and the difficulties with open
arms, because if God has allowed it all, it's for the purpose of
our edification and salvation. Never forget friend, every tear,
hurt, pain and anguishing moment you have suffered has prepared you for this specific moment. God wants you to know
that he entrusted you with a specific assignment that only you
could accomplish; therefore your preparation had to be meticulously designed by Him. That is why he allowed the misery

and distress to envelope you—it was your incubator. You are now ready to soar as He has predestined!

Discussion Questions for Chapter 9

1. Point out the similarities between a faithful believer and the honey badger.
2. Can you answer the famous question, "Why me?"
3. What do the venomous bee stings represent?
4. What similarities are there between the fight between the honey badger and the cobra, and the fight between the believer and the enemy?
5. What benefit is produced with every tear you shed?
6. What is the antidote?
7. How has God used this book for your restoration and resurrection?

About the Author

Mark Vega is a preacher who travels and proclaims the message of salvation and hope throughout the nations. He is passionate about seeing people experience the salvation of their souls and restoration in their lives, and he loves seeing the church be empowered to succeed and to make a difference. Mark is unique among preachers for his ability to communicate both in English and in Spanish God's message to leaders, adults, and youth. His ministry ties cultures together and calls people to encounter Christ. Mark Vega is the founder of IGNITE Inc., an internship program that prepares young people called to full-time ministry in the areas of leadership and ministerial life. Responding to God's call on his life, Rev. Vega left his professional career for a full-time pursuit of his preaching and Bible teaching ministry. Mark and Lisa Vega are the pastors of Ignite Life Center, a vibrant and growing church in Gainesville, Florida.

For more information about Pastor Vega's ministry visit
www.markvega.org.

For more information on the Ministry Training Center visit
www.Ignite.org.

Ignite...

GOD'S HEART FOR A NEW GENERATION

Our **goal** in the internership program is to Ignite the distinct call of God in the lives of our students.

One of the most exciting, biblically-based training programs that incorporates training, practical experience and one-to-one mentorship for young people who want to impact their world with God's help and anointing.

If you are considering training and/or have a friend interested, check us out first ... **you won't be disappointed!**

Visit us at **www.ignite.org**